KITCHEN TABLE B

ELIJAH AND ELISHA

All of Me
for
All of Jesus

BY BETH COPPEDGE

EDITED BY CRICKET ALBERTSON

TABLE OF CONTENTS

Dedication 4

Foreword 5

1. Providence University 7

2. All of Me for All of Him 31

3. The Restoration of God 53

4. Squeaky Clean Hearts 79

5. Planning Funerals or Resurrections 101

6. A Transformed Heart / A Covetous Heart 123

7. The Three Mini-Miracles 153

8. In Times of Famine 181

9. Victory..201

10. Holy and Blameless 223

Endnotes 231

DEDICATION

To Al Coppedge,
my precious husband, who took Jesus' command to
make disciples as his life's mission.
His commitment and passion captivated my heart
and compelled me to join him in calling others to be
disciples of Jesus.

FOREWORD

We are so excited that you have decided to join us as we study the lives of Elijah and Elisha. The beauty of studying God's Word is that God always speaks, and His Word never returns void (Isaiah 55:10-11). In fact, in the last letter that the Apostle Paul wrote to his young friend Timothy, he stressed the incredible value of Scripture, even from childhood, to make us wise for salvation through faith in Jesus Christ (2 Timothy 3:15-17). If we are to be thoroughly equipped to allow God to fulfill His purposes in our lives, we must become ardent students of God's Word.

After my husband, Al, and I were married we waited upon Jesus for direction for our lives. We felt God calling us to teach the Word and to disciple men and women in the gospel of Jesus Christ. Al felt led to the mandate in 2 Timothy 2:2, and since that time he has faithfully been teaching and discipling students as a seminary professor. My heart felt drawn to Titus 2:3-5. I began to teach the Word and mentor women from our home—from my kitchen table, so to speak—as a wife, mom and now a grandmother.

The mandate for Titus Women is to share the message of the Holy Heart, loving Jesus with all one's heart, mind and strength (Deuteronomy 6:6). Titus 2:3-5 calls older women in the faith to train younger ones in a love relationship that transforms all areas of life. This is an incredible life calling to "Titus" (a synonym for the verb "disciple") not only our physical progeny, but our spiritual as well.

All the women involved in Titus Women believe that God is raising us up together to share Jesus and make Him known. Our motto is, "In Him and In Each Other to Reach the World for Jesus Christ." Some of the team are older, some younger, but all are lovers of Jesus and long to make His goodness known. We hope the whole concept of sharing Him together as a team will challenge you to also become a "Titus Woman" and you will begin to ask Jesus to help you invest your life for Jesus into others. If you ask Him, He will begin to lay certain people on your heart to pray over and to carry so that the life of Jesus might become a living reality in them. It is a marvelous way to live—investing in eternity.

One of the best ways to disciple other women is by studying God's Word together. Studying the Word allows us to know our Triune God: Father, Son and Holy Spirit. When this happens, transformation always occurs! We get a feel for the joy that such transformation brings in Isaiah 55:12-13: "You shall go out with joy and be led forth in peace; the mountains and the hills shall break forth into singing before you. And all the trees of the field shall clap their hands. Instead of the thorn shall come up the cypress tree, and instead of the brier shall come up the myrtle. It shall be to the Lord for a name, for an everlasting sign that shall not be cut off."

When we know Jesus and His Word abides in us, "we go forth with joy and are led forth with peace." What exuberance and joy come to our lives when we make Christ the center and when we know His Word! He even transforms difficulties into beauty and knowledge.

You are in our hearts and prayers as you begin the study of Elijah and Elisha. Any time we study God's Word, it brings Him joy. You are making His heart sing.

–Beth Coppedge

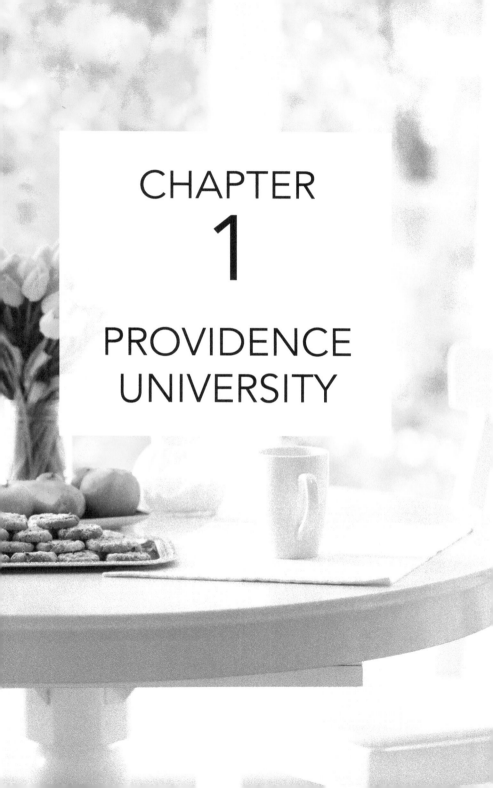

CHAPTER

1

PROVIDENCE
UNIVERSITY

I love the mystery characters in Scripture. Elijah is one of these. Suddenly, he appears on the pages of the Biblical story without any background or warning. We know that he is a Tishbite, but scholars are not even sure where Tishbi is. We know that he is from Gilead on the east side of the Jordan. Gilead is a rocky, hilly, barren country, and it seems fitting that the solitary and courageous prophet of Yahweh would come from such a desolate place. We get the impression that Gilead, like Galilee to Nathaniel, implies the question, "Can anything good come from there?" (John 1:46). From this barren place, the God of Israel lifts a leader to challenge the people of God in a very dark and apostate hour. The word of the Lord comes to Elijah with authority, and Elijah simply repeats God's message to King Ahab:

> *And Elijah, the Tishbite, of the inhabitants of Gilead, said to Ahab, "As the Lord God lives before whom I stand, there shall not be dew nor rain these years except at my word."*
>
> *Then the word of the Lord came to him saying, "Get away from here, turn eastward, and hide by the brook Cherith, which flows into the Jordan, and it will be that you will drink from the brook. And I have commanded the ravens to feed you there." So he went and did according to all that the word of the Lord said. For he went and he stayed by the brook Cherith which flows into the Jordan. The ravens brought him bread and*

meat in the morning and bread and meat in the evening, and he drank from the brook. And it happened after a while, that the brook dried up because there had been no rain in the land (1 Kings 17:1-7).

A Nation in Moral Bankruptcy

The nation of Israel had reached a state of moral bankruptcy. Ahab, the reigning king, had gone to Phoenicia and brought home a queen named Jezebel, one of the most notorious women in all human history. Jezebel was not a follower of Yahweh, the God of Israel. She worshipped Baal and brought the worship of Baal into Israel. Ahab established his capital in Samaria, and in order to please his wife, he built a temple to Baal. In addition to building a temple for a foreign deity, he attempted to merge the religion of Israel and the worship of Baal into one. He wanted to synchronize the faith of God's people with the faith of his new wife. Not only that, Ahab rebuilt the city of Jericho which God had commanded never to be rebuilt. He built it at Bethel which is where Yahweh had met Jacob with the dream of the ladder from heaven to earth. This was a holy place to the people of God, but Ahab built on this site the city of Jericho, and in order to have the blessing of (all) the gods on it, he sacrificed his two sons and built their bodies into the wall and into the gate. He felt that the only way he could have the blessing was to sacrifice his sons. The wickedness of Israel had reached a new level of corruption. The people of Israel followed the example of their king and queen in their licentious, violent, and immoral behavior. Ahab had the disastrous notion that he could have Yahweh *plus*. Yahweh *plus* Baal, Yahweh *plus* the approval of his pagan wife, Yahweh *plus* financial blessing.

Recently, I received a phone call from a friend, and she said to me, "Do you know what? I am so tired of destination theology!"

And I said, "What do you mean?"

"I mean the kind of Christianity where we say a simple little prayer and then think that we have fire insurance, so we can live however we want to live. It is a lie, straight from hell."

I agree with my friend. Any Christian theology that allows us to have Jesus *plus* is simply not true. God is not looking for *destination theology*; he is looking for *transformation theology*, where we come under the knife of the cross, and God can transform us. The word *transform* means to *metamorphose*, like a caterpillar turning into a butterfly. God wants to change us and make us people after His own heart, with white hot hearts for God.

> *God wants to change us and make us people after His own heart.*

Yahweh, the true God of Israel, is not willing to be mixed with anything else. He is God, and He stands alone in every human life. At this point, it looked like the evil one would completely wipe out the people of God, but God had another idea. Like with Hannah and her desire for a son, God worked with one individual to bring His message to the people of God.

God Looks for One

God does not need five hundred people to make a difference in His world. He does not need a hundred thousand people. He simply needs one, and He found one in the prophet Elijah. Elijah was willing to stand alone for God; he was willing to walk with God and to obey God's directions, no matter how crazy they seemed to be.

What made Elijah's life distinct?

Elijah was a man who lived in the presence of Yahweh and had the character of Yahweh. He was holy; he lived a blameless life before God. The character and nature of the God of Israel is holiness. Holiness is mentioned in the Old Testament 890 times; it is used 157 times in the book of Leviticus. God wanted to teach His people what it meant for them to live holy lives, set apart for God. In the Pentateuch, God organized a people group, and then He instructed them to be holy even as He is holy. They were to look like their God in their character, their behavior, and their nature.

God does not need five hundred people to make a difference in His world. He does not need a hundred thousand people. He simply needs one.

The difference between Biblical faith and the culture that surrounded Israel or the culture around us today is holiness. The God and Father of Jesus Christ has called His people to a life in which they are set apart for Himself. Elijah was set apart for the purposes of God, and as believers we enter a covenant relationship with the eternal God through the precious presence of Jesus Christ. He enters a human life through His own grace and our faith, not through works or human righteousness. When believers in Christ are indwelt through His Holy Spirit, He transforms us to look more and more like the heavenly Father. This covenantal relationship is one in which "all of me is given for all of Jesus." An exchange is made, and His presence is given. Then the transformation of character begins!

In this relationship of love, God begins to spell out in a person's life what it means to walk before Him and "be blameless," so that the double-mindedness is gone, and a person's will is simply to will the will of the Father, no matter what it costs. In the secular society of our world, religion usually is another means of getting personal needs met. A covenantal life of love, exchange, and obedience is neither accepted nor welcomed. In the pagan world of Ahab's day, religion was simply a means of manipulating the physical universe to accomplish one's own personal goals. In our society, this is also how we use Christianity many times. We want our children to do well or we want financial blessing or physical healing, and so we go through the motions of "faith" in order to receive the gifts of God's blessing. This is not a Christian worldview. Anytime we want to control God and control our circumstances, we have stepped out of a covenant relationship with the covenant-keeping God and moved into a man-made religious form.

God offers to His people a relationship of intimacy, in which we can know the eternal God and

> *God offers to His people a relationship of intimacy, in which we can know the eternal God and be known by Him.*

be known by Him. As we enter this covenant, we begin to desire more and more of Him and we begin to look more and more like Him, through the power of the Spirit whom He gives to anyone who will ask. God is looking to transform His people; He wants to take the old and make it something new and beautiful.

Providence University

When Elijah came to the people of God, he brought a word of judgment from Yahweh: there would be a famine. Sometimes into the life of His creatures, God sends circumstances so difficult that the only hope is to look beyond human help to God and God alone. He desires to force His people to stop trying to meet their needs in their own strength, to look to Him for help, and to acknowledge Him as God. God's message to Ahab was a message of judgment, and God sent his message through Elijah, but then in an incredibly unexpected turn of events, God took this prophet, and He set him aside in an out of the way place for an extended period.

The eternal God said to Elijah, "Get away from here and turn eastward, and hide by the Brook Cherith, which flows into the Jordan which flows into the Jordan. And it will be *that* you shall drink from the brook, and I have commanded the ravens to feed you there." (I Kings 17:3-4). Just when it seemed that God was going to give Elijah a real platform for ministry, God sent him to the backside of the wilderness to sit by a brook and be fed by the birds. I read an old commentary by a camp meeting preacher, and he said that God was enrolling Elijah in *Providence University*; God would teach him things here that never could have been taught in Samaria.

Lesson #1: The Lesson of Peril & Protection

Some of the most difficult challenges for the people of God come when He takes His followers abruptly and unexpectedly out of the line of fire and enrolls them in Providence University, out of the way and out of the limelight. Often this comes just as we might have expected a breakthrough, an open door or a window of opportunity, and then we find ourselves shut up again with God and God alone. The first lesson God taught the prophet in Providence U was that when God gives direction, He will also give provision and protection. If the direction is difficult, it is safe to obey in faith; the God of Israel will provide for His students. When we first hear the instructions God gives, we might respond with:

When God gives direction, He will also give provision and protection.

"Surely God, this could not be what you have for me. I am hidden away here by myself."

"This is not what I envisioned for my life."

"I wanted you to USE me!"

"How can I flourish in the desert?"

"I don't want this!"

We do not actually know if Elijah thought or said any of those things, but I know I would have! Elijah heard God's instructions, he obeyed His voice, and he waited for God's provision. As Elijah waited, God began to develop in him patience, humility, and trust in a way that could never have been done if Elijah was in the spotlight.

As God's people begin to be patient in the little things that God brings into our lives, even in the circumstances that are not to our liking, we learn and grow. If we submit to the dealings of God at Providence University, He can begin to grow us and transform us in ways we could never imagine. Like Elijah, at the end of our season of being tucked away, God will be able to accomplish His purposes through our lives without self getting in the way. When God redirects us, often He wants to move us into purposeful solitude. In the lives of every true follower of Christ, there are times when God forces us into seasons of solitude, so that we can deal with God and God alone. When we begin to find out who we are in loneliness, we begin to understand who He is. Then, He has the freedom to transform our hearts and set us free from pride and self-sufficiency.

Be thankful for the needs of today and trust God for the provision for tomorrow.

During this season Elijah was protected—from crazy kings and queens, from political disturbance, and even from famine. God provided for him. The ravens brought him food regularly, but Elijah had to learn to wait for the provision and accept it from the beaks of the ravens. He had to trust God for provision every single day, morning and night, from very odd messengers. It is hard for us to live one day at a time, trusting God for day-by-day provision. We end up worrying about lack or feeling guilty about using what we have. God taught Elijah to be thankful for the needs of today and trust God for the provision for tomorrow.

I heard a story that perfectly illustrates God's provision when we trust Him. There was a family who found Christ and felt called to go into ministry. They had two children, Paul and Ruth, and the father had a good job at a machinery company. He resigned his position, and they left everything to go to Bible school. As he got ready to leave, his boss told him that if he ever changed his mind, he would have a job at that company. They went to Bible school, and a day came when they had no more money. They had used all their savings, and they did not have enough money to even go grocery shopping. They walked the kids to the drugstore and bought them candy bars for breakfast because all they had was some change. As they were walking home, the father looked at his wife and said, "Honey, I think we have made a mistake. God must not have been in this decision. I am going to return to my old job."

Their Heavenly Father had seen their plight and had fed them.

That little wife had developed a habit of quiet time. She sought God carefully every day, and she said to her husband. "Could we just wait one more day and see what Jesus will do?"

Quietly her husband agreed, "One more day, but I can't let my family go hungry. That wouldn't honor Jesus." They walked home and unlocked the door, and there sitting on the table were bags of groceries. Opening the refrigerator, they found it fully stocked with food. The ravens had come to feed them; they never knew who brought the food to them, only that their Heavenly Father had seen their plight, and had fed them.

Learning to trust God in all circumstances is a life of increasing freedom and joy. Elijah knew how to wait on God for His provision.

Lesson #2: The Lesson of Poverty & Provision

Even the great prophet Elijah had to have lessons in faith, and God began to teach Elijah another lesson, even more challenging to his faith than the first one:

> *Then the word of the Lord came again to him and said, "Arise, and go to Zarephath which belongs to Sidon and dwell there. See I have commanded a widow there to provide for you." So, he arose, and he went to Zarephath. And then he came to the gate of the city, indeed a widow was there gathering sticks. And he called to her, "Oh please bring me a little water in a cup that I may drink." And as she was going to do it, he said to her, "Could you please bring me a morsel of bread in your hand as well."*
>
> *"Oh," she said, "as the Lord your God lives, I do not have bread; only a handful of flour in a bin and a little oil in a jar. And see, I am gathering a couple of sticks that I may go and prepare it for myself and my son that we may eat it and die."*
>
> *And Elijah said, "Do not fear. Go and do as I say. Bring me a small cake from it first. And afterward bake some for yourself and your son, for thus says the Lord, God of Israel, 'The bin of flour shall not be used up, nor shall the jar of oil run dry until the day the Lord sends rain on the earth.'" So, she went away and did according to the word of Elijah. And she and her household ate for many days. The*

bin of flour was not used up nor did the oil run dry according to the word of the Lord which he spoke to Elijah.

In Providence University, the lessons became increasingly difficult as the Brook Cherith began to evaporate. Can you imagine Elijah's inner panic as he watched his little water supply dwindle away? I am sure the evil one was sitting there whispering thoughts of doubt and depression into his mind. I am sure there was a temptation to run away, but God held him steady, and Elijah trusted Him again. Elijah stayed until God spoke to him.

Elijah did not listen to the lies of the enemy, and we do not have to either.

There are times in believers' lives when we watch the resources of God dry right up, and it looks as if God has abandoned us and left us in a dark night of the soul. The temptation for Christians at that point is to start accusing God.

"God, where are you?"

"Do you realize the pain I am in?"

"Do you realize the underpinnings of my life have been destroyed?"

"Do you care if we perish?"

"All I want to do is serve you, to be yours, to be blameless. I have surrendered everything, and this is what you do with my life?"

Elijah did not listen to the lies of the enemy, and we do not have to either. Elijah waited on the word of the Lord.

Then God spoke to Elijah, "Your time at the Brook Cherith is over (thankfully, because the brook was gone). Go to Zarephath." I am sure after the initial relief, Elijah faced the reality that Zarephath was not an ideal location for a runaway prophet. It was right in the middle of Jezebel's country. I can imagine that Elijah tried to argue with the Lord, "I cannot go into her country. She is seeking my life to kill me. I am on the most-wanted list."

God asked, "Elijah, are you going to trust me in places of danger? Just like you trusted me in places of scarcity and loneliness? Do you believe I am big enough to take care of you even if there is physical danger?"

The name Zarephath meant *The Smelting Furnace*. Hot, miserable, and dangerous. God is not sending Elijah into a green pasture; God directed him into a dark and dangerous place. Willingly, Elijah obeyed the voice of Yahweh, and God promised him that a widow in Zarephath would provide for his needs. The funny thing was that the widow does not seem to realize she was intended to take care of this shaggy looking man who appeared out of the wilderness and asked her for bread and water. God required Elijah to trust Him, and He also required the little widow to trust Him.

"Ma'am, could you please bring me a little cup of water?"

"Yes," she said as she gathered twigs to make a fire.

"Would you give me a little bread as well?"

"Mister, I would like to bring you food, but I am preparing the last food my son and I have. We are going to eat it and die."

Audaciously Elijah said, "Go, make a cake for me first, and then go and make one for you and your son. God has told me that your oil will not dry up and your flour barrel will not be empty until this famine is over because of your generosity to me."

It is difficult to trust God to provide for our needs, but it is even more difficult to trust Him to provide through other people. This level of trust requires a humility and a dependence against which the natural human spirit rebels. Despite that, Elijah trusted, and this woman trusted and gave the last bit that she had to Elijah. When she went back to her kitchen after feeding him his small cake, there was a little more flour in the bin. God's provision continued until the famine ended. He provided for her daily needs so that she could provide for Elijah. Just like He provided for Elijah by Cherith, now two other persons were enrolled in Providence University, trusting God to take care of all three of them. God always has a way to take care of his own, but he cannot take care of us if we try to help him out. We have to trust Him completely.

> *God always has a way to take care of His own, but he cannot take care of us if we try to help Him out. We have to trust Him completely.*

I read Corrie Ten Boom's *The Hiding Place*.[1] Corrie and her sister, Betsy, were prisoners in the deadly concentration camp in Germany, Ravensbruck. When they arrived at Ravensbruck, all prisoners had to turn in their belongings; Betsy and Corrie prayed and asked God to protect the few treasures they had: a Bible, vitamin drops, and a blue sweater to keep Betsy warm. Going into the shower room, Corrie stowed their few belongings under a bench and then after her shower, she tucked them down under her new prison uniform. God protected their few things, and together with their few supplies they ended up in the miserable Barracks 28, where five women slept per bed, with hundreds of women in the large room, and eight overflowing toilets in the middle. Betsy looked at Corrie, and then whispered, "Jesus, how will we live?" Then she looked at Corrie and said, "Read me the passage we read last night from I Thessalonians 5, where it says, "Rejoice always, pray without ceasing, in everything give thanks."

"Give thanks, Corrie. That is what Jesus wants us to do." Betsy began to pray, and she began to give thanks. Her thankful heart attracted other women. Every night women gathered around their bunk as they read their Scriptures. Corrie said the Word of God seemed to be so real and true, it was as if the ink was not quite dry. After reading together, Betsy shared her vitamin drops with all the women. Corrie did not like that at all because Betsy needed them so badly, but Betsy was determined, and so they shared. Night after night, those little drops were doled out to needy and desperate women. One day, a guard who was an undercover friend came into the barracks and whispered to Corrie and Betsy, "Look what I have: a whole bottle of vitamins!" She gave them to the sisters to be distributed to others. That night, Corrie said, "I will just finish up the last drop of vitamin oil before we open the new bottle," but no more drops came out. She shook and squeezed, but not another drop came from that vitamin bottle. God's new provision replaced the old in perfect sequence.

We can know His provision in the same way that Betsy and Corrie knew it, as we look to Him and trust Him and learn the lesson of God's provision in places of poverty.

Lesson #3 —The Lesson of Pressure & Prevailing Prayer

Elijah learned the lessons of the brook and the lessons of the widow, but the intensity of Providence University did not go away. In fact, the lessons kept increasing in difficulty and the need for faith:

> *Now it happened after these things that the son of the woman of the house became sick, and his sickness was so serious that there was no breath in him. She said to Elijah, "What have I to do with you, Oh man of God? Have you come to me to bring my sin to remembrance and to kill my son?"*
>
> *He said to her, "Give me your son." So, he took him out of her arms and took him to the upper room where he was staying, and he laid the child on his bed. Then he cried out to the Lord and said, "O Lord, my God, have you brought tragedy on this widow with whom I lodge by killing her son?" And he stretched himself out on the child three times and cried out to the Lord and said, "O Lord, my God, I pray, let this child's soul come back to him." Then the Lord heard the voice of Elijah, and the soul of the child came back to him, and he revived. And Elijah took the child and brought him down from the upper room into the house and gave him to his mother. And Elijah said, "See, the child lives!"*

Then the woman said to Elijah, "Now by this I know that you are a man of God, and that the word of the Lord in your mouth is the truth" (1 Kings 17:17-24).

This place of Zarephath proved to be a place of peril and poverty, but then, pressure was added to the mix. Elijah found himself responsible for a widow and her son. The son of that courageous little woman died, and the woman came to him in anger. "Why did you come and take my son? You make me think of all my sins."

Elijah was horrified, and he responded, "Give me your son." Then, he took the little guy up to his room, turned to Yahweh and says, "God, why have you killed the widow's son?" The pressure intensified, and Elijah knew where to go—straight to the heart of God. Elijah cried out to the Lord for mercy, "Let this child's soul come back to him." Elijah travailed in prayer! In the place of incredible pressure, poverty, and peril, Elijah entered into prevailing prayer. When Elijah did not know what else to do because of the difficulty of the circumstances God allowed in his life, he began to pray, and he did not stop until God answered. The faith of the woman was at stake, and the life of the child was at stake. Elijah laid on that child's face and breathed life into him and prayed, "Oh God, let this child's soul come back." God heard the cry of that man's heart, and the boy's spirit came back and entered that child. Elijah took the child to his mother and presented him alive: "Behold, here is your son."

> *God is inviting His people to enter prevailing prayer on behalf of children, spouses, communities, and nations.*

The mother of that boy looked at the prophet in awe and said, "Truly, I know, you are a man of God." Truly, he was.

In 1 Kings 17, Elijah entered Providence University with God and waited on God to teach him all God wanted him to learn. He held on instead of giving up. He held steady instead of going home. He trusted instead of questioning, and he prayed instead of going into despair. God is inviting His people to enter prevailing prayer on behalf of children, spouses, communities, and nations. We must be people who will allow God to bring us to Cherith, people that allow God to take us to Zarephath, and people that will prevail in prayer for those God has laid on our hearts.

> *He held on instead of giving up. He held steady instead of going home. He trusted instead of questioning, and he prayed instead of going into despair.*

Hard? Yes! Blessed? Yes!! We find a joy comes when we participate in God's purposes for His world. We begin to know God Himself, know His heart, not just know about Him but know who He is, and the power and presence of Jesus begins to rest on our lives. God has freedom to move through our lives through the power of the Holy Spirit.

Why do so few people prevail in prayer?

The problem is that we are lazy, and prayer is costly. Frankly, we do not really want to know Him because it means that we will have to change, and change requires courage and trust. It cost Jesus everything for you and for me, and if we are going to walk the way of Jesus, we will have to get to the place where it is not us, it is Him. It is not what I want, it is what He wants. In this place we begin to really live, and out of our lives the redemptive blood of Jesus begins to flow to touch a world for God, to touch a nation for God, to touch states for God, to touch homes for God, to touch ministries for God, to touch marriages for God, to touch children (born and unborn) for God.

The story of the family who had to feed their children candy bars for breakfast continues. God called the mom and dad to take their family to the Middle East as missionaries, and so they obeyed and went. Every Friday night, the parents would fast and pray for the work of God to be done in their place of ministry. While they fasted, the mama would make the children cinnamon rice for supper, which was their favorite food. Paul and Ruth remembered Friday nights as the happiest night of the week, and the idea of prayer and fasting had the happiest memories associated with it. When Paul was old enough, he went to a Christian college, and God began to place a call on his life to go into missions. Eventually, God called him to start a radio program that could be broadcasted into communist and Islamic nations. His parents came to help him with the launch of the radio station, and they found one day that there was no more money to continue. They began to pray, and while they prayed, Paul got a phone call from a friend who was passing through town. He invited Paul to come and have lunch with him. While they were eating together, the friend looked at him and said, "I was not going to tell you this yet, but our church just voted to fully underwrite the new radio ministry." Then, he handed Paul a check, hopped on the train and was gone. Out of the prevailing prayers of a mother and a father and two children, Trans-World Radio was birthed, and eighty-five to ninety percent of the world has access to the Gospel of Jesus through that radio. A father and mother who made prayer night the happiest night of the week produced a son who prevailed in prayer until God broke through with His provision.

> *Will we let God become our teacher in protection, provision, and prevailing prayer?*

At some point, every Christian who is wholly following God will find himself or herself enrolled in Providence University. The question is, will we let God become our teacher in protection, provision, and prevailing prayer? God can teach any willing and open heart that looks to Him in trust and obedience.

Personal Reflection

Have you seen God provide for you in creative ways? Are you trusting Him enough to allow miracle stories in your life or do you always have to be in control?

Has God ever pulled you out of the spotlight and hidden you away? What has been your response? Why does God allow this? What was He trying to teach in your life?

What do we do when our obedience to Jesus Christ imposes on someone else? If this happens, do we pull back or press in to Christ and trust?

Notes

Notes

Notes

_____
_____
_____
_____
_____
_____
_____
_____
_____
_____
_____
_____
_____
_____
_____
_____
_____
_____
_____
_____
_____
_____
_____
_____
_____
_____
_____
_____
_____
_____

CHAPTER
2

ALL OF ME FOR
ALL OF HIM

*D*rumroll please…prepare for one of the most dramatic chapters in all of Scripture. In 1 Kings 18, Elijah, the prophet of Israel's God, Yahweh, challenged the four hundred and fifty prophets of Jezebel's God, Baal, to a face-to-face confrontation. In a massive showdown, one man stood against many and called on his God to prove Himself to His own people. Not many people have the courage to force God to prove Himself, but Elijah fearlessly stood before the people of Israel and said, "If Yahweh is God, worship Him! If Baal is God, worship Him! Whichever God answers, that God is the one, true, and living God."

This is the kind of challenge which would make believers shudder and cringe with this simple question, "What if the true God does not answer?" Elijah had no such fears. He knew his God, and he knew that God would show up and prove Himself to His own people. The story is full of suspense, danger, and emotion, but before this great confrontation, the writer of 1 Kings gives a glimpse into the hearts of those involved at Mount Carmel. Three character studies of different men with three radically different hearts illustrate the real issue before the people of God. What is the state of one's heart? Only then does the larger story unfold.

> *And it came to pass after many days that the word of the Lord came to Elijah, in the third year, saying, "Go, present yourself to Ahab, and I will send rain on the earth."*
>
> *Elijah went to present himself to Ahab; and there was a severe famine in Samaria. And Ahab*

had called Obadiah, who oversaw his house. (Now Obadiah feared the Lord greatly. For so it was, while Jezebel massacred the prophets of the Lord, that Obadiah had taken one hundred prophets and hidden them, fifty to a cave, and had fed them with bread and water.) And Ahab had said to Obadiah, "Go into the land to all the springs of water and to all the brooks; perhaps we may find grass to keep the horses and mules alive, so that we will not have to kill any live-stock." So they divided the land between them to explore it; Ahab went one way by himself, and Obadiah went another way by himself.

Now as Obadiah was on his way, suddenly Elijah met him; and he recognized him, and fell on his face, and said, "Is that you, my lord Elijah?" And he answered him, "It is I. Go, tell your master, 'Elijah is here.'"

So he said, "How have I sinned, that you are delivering your servant into the hand of Ahab, to kill me? As the Lord your God lives, there is no nation or kingdom where my master has not sent someone to hunt for you; and when they said, 'He is not here,' he took an oath from the kingdom or nation that they could not find you. And now you say, 'Go, tell your master, Elijah is here!' And it shall come to pass, as soon as I am gone from you, that the Spirit of the Lord will carry you to a place I do not know; so when I go and tell Ahab, and he cannot find you, he will kill me."

…. Then Elijah said, "As the Lord of hosts lives, before whom I stand, I will surely present myself to him today."

So, Obadiah went to meet Ahab, and told him; and Ahab went to meet Elijah.

Then it happened, when Ahab saw Elijah that Ahab said to him, "Is that you, O troubler of Israel?"

And he answered, "I have not troubled Israel, but you and your father's house in that you have forsaken the commandments of the Lord and followed the Baals" (1 Kings 18:1-18).

An Undivided Heart

Elijah had been staying with the widow in Zarephath, and after many days, the Word of the Lord came again to Elijah, giving him instruction that it was time to act. As soon as the Word of God came to Elijah, he obeyed. He did not initiate the activity, but he waited on God and then acted in obedience when God spoke. Elijah lived in total dependence on God and in utmost obedience to God, even when he did not fully understand the purpose of God's word to him. He lived one big "yes" to the will of God. Because of his willingness to trust God and obey Him implicitly, God lovingly cared for him even under harsh circumstances. The one that trusts the will of God even when it is not easily understood is the one for whom God

The one that trusts the will of God even when it is not easily understood is the one for whom God delights to care.

delights to care. That was the state of Elijah's heart. His heart was undivided in his love and loyalty to Yahweh. He did not go back and forth between obedience and disobedience; he did not compromise with sin and evil. He simply listened to the voice of Yahweh and then obeyed. His heart was undivided, constant, full of faith and love.

A Divided Heart

The second man in 1 Kings 18 is not Ahab but Ahab's assistant, Obadiah. The way Obadiah is described in Scripture is unusual because some of the things that are said are extremely positive and others are equally negative. The Biblical record does not give us a straightforward answer when it comes to the question of Obadiah's heart.

First, Obadiah was the head of Ahab's household. *A definite negative.*

Second, Obadiah feared the Lord. *A definite positive.*

Third, Obadiah hid one hundred of the Lord's prophets so they would not be killed by Jezebel. *Okay, that is good.*

Fourth, Obadiah is terrified to tell Ahab about Elijah. *Negative.*

Fear dominated Obadiah's life. Obadiah was jittery, anxious, afraid, and divided—a man who rode the fence, a man of compromise, a man who was most concerned about his own well-being and security. He was willing to do right if it was not wrong for his own best interest. He wanted God, but he also wanted to be in control, and he was not quite sure about the trustworthiness of God. As a result, he was a nervous wreck. Elijah was bold, fearless, and obedient. Obadiah was cowardly, fearful, and anxious.

The hardest thing in the world is to live with a divided heart: half for self and half for God. Instead of ever selling out to the full will of God, Obadiah tried to honor God and take care of himself at the same time. In every life, God will sooner or later make life difficult enough that we can no longer live in both realities, and we will have to make a choice. Elijah showed up and confronted Obadiah, "Would you tell Ahab that I am here?" For the next six verses, Obadiah whined and argued with Elijah, "I cannot do that. I will be killed!" His top priority was not the will of Yahweh; it was not the good of God's people; it was his own safety and well-being. Anytime we make ourselves our ultimate concern, we will live in fear and trembling.

> *The hardest thing in the world is to live with a divided heart: half for self and half for God.*

A Self-Centered Heart and An Evil Heart

Finally, Ahab appears again in the story, the man who accommodated evil to such an extent that he wedded himself to one of the most wicked women in human history. Jezebel sold herself to do evil. Ahab did not want to do evil himself, he just married someone who would do it for him. She killed the prophets.

She killed Naboth in order to steal his vineyard. Ahab accommodated evil if it worked to his own advantage, and if good ever benefited him, he would accommodate that as well. Ahab placed Obadiah as the head of his household. He knew that Obadiah had helped the prophets of Yahweh, and he wanted some of Yahweh's followers in his house too. He knew he would rather have a partial God-follower as the head of his home than a cutthroat like his own wife. Ahab used the people in his life for his own personal advantage—whether evil or good, and in the process, he lost his own soul and became evil himself. When he confronted Elijah, he accused him of causing Israel's trouble, when it was his own actions which had sunk the country into famine and disarray.

Reading to the end of the story is always interesting. Scripture records very different destinies for these men. The one man who was always saying "yes" to the will of God, who lived in obedience to Him, ends up in glory, taken into the presence of God in a fiery chariot, like no other person who ever lived. We read of Elijah on the Mount of Transfiguration talking to Jesus, the Son of God. He ministered to Jesus Himself and became the prototype of the Messiah. He stood for truth, for Yahweh, even when he had to stand alone. The end of Elijah's story was one of glory and honor.

The end of Obadiah's story is absent. After this chapter, we never hear of Obadiah again. Scripture is silent about this double-minded man. His story fades into oblivion without distinction or value.

Ahab's story ended with violence and horror; both he and Jezebel die violent deaths, and every single child and grandchild of theirs was destroyed. His story came to a gruesome and tragic end. Tolerating evil caused evil for generations and generations. The words of the Lord in Deuteronomy to Moses became hauntingly real and true:

> *And it shall be that if you earnestly obey My commandments which I command you today, to love the Lord your God and serve Him with all your heart and with all your soul, then I will give you the rain for your land in its season....Take heed to yourselves, lest your heart be deceived, and you turn aside and serve other gods and worship them, lest the Lord's anger be aroused against you, and He shut up the heavens so that there be no rain, and the land yield no produce, and you perish quickly from the good land the Lord is giving you (Deuteronomy 11:13-17).*

The Challenge

The nation of Israel had gone the way of Ahab; they accommodated evil and were being destroyed. The pain of the severe famine had grown so intense that God's people had to confront their relationship to Yahweh. This is exactly what God tries to do in the life of His people today. He lets the difficulty get great enough that we must confront who He is and our relationship to Him. Pain, famine, unmet needs (emotionally or physically), and heart longings all become the means God uses to get our attention. God gets His people to the place of desperation, and then they are forced to confront their relationship to Him, just as He did in I Kings 18:19-24 when Elijah said to Ahab:

> Send and gather all Israel to me on Mount Carmel, the four hundred and fifty prophets of Baal, and the four hundred prophets of Asherah, who eat at Jezebel's table.

So Ahab sent for all the children of Israel, and
gathered the prophets together on Mount
Carmel. And Elijah came to all the people, and
said, "How long will you falter between two
opinions? If the Lord is God, follow Him; but if
Baal, follow him." But the people answered him
not a word.

Then Elijah said to the people, "I alone am left
a prophet of the Lord; but Baal's prophets are
four hundred and fifty men. Therefore, let them
give us two bulls; and let them choose one bull
for themselves, cut it in pieces, and lay it on the
wood, but put no fire under it. Then you call
on the name of your gods, and I will call on the
name of the Lord; and the God who answers by
fire, He is God."

The people of Israel agreed to Elijah's proposal,
and the prophets of Baal began to build their altar and
prepare it for a sacrifice. They placed the bull upon
the altar and danced around the sacrifice, ranting,
railing, and wounding themselves "until the blood
flowed." They called in desperation and cried from
morning until evening, but even with all their effort
and pleadings, no fire came.

Finally, Elijah's turn came. When evening fell,
Elijah courageously called the people of Israel near
and began to work. Elijah spent a long time preparing
the altar and the sacrifice. He rebuilt the broken altar
of Yahweh, placed the sacrifice on it, and then he dug
a trench all around it. Three times he drenched the
entire altar with water. The prayer that Elijah prayed
after the sacrifice was complete was compelling in
its simplicity, "Hear me, Oh Lord, hear me. That this
people may know You, and that you are the Lord God,

and that You have turned their hearts back to you again" (18:37).

Then, the fire came—straight from heaven! It consumed the sacrifice, the altar, the stones and the trench around it. No one could doubt: God Himself came to Mount Carmel the way He had come to Mount Sinai, with fire and with power: "Then the fire of the Lord fell and consumed the burnt sacrifice, and the wood and the stones and the dust, and it licked up the water that was in the trench. Now when all the people saw it, they fell on their faces, and they said, 'The Lord, He is God! The Lord, He is God!'" (18:38-39).

God's presence comes with power, and He gives us His power to begin to live day-by-day in His life-giving presence.

The living God of Elijah made Himself known in power, and the people's response was one of purity and piety. They destroyed the prophets of Baal and committed themselves to the worship of Yahweh.

When God makes Himself known, He causes a determination to set our faces to follow Him and Him alone; He brings purity and cleanses every part of our hearts; and He gives power to rid our lives of any evil that we have allowed to enter in. Sin is like cancer; if we allow one small sin it can eat us alive, consuming our souls, our families, and our lives. God's presence makes us "squeaky clean." God's presence comes with power, and He gives us His power to begin to live day-by-day in His life-giving presence.

Power does not always come in signs and wonders; sometimes it comes in a sweet spirit with our families during the busy and stressful dinner hour. Power means that we can put someone's needs above our own. Power means we can lay down our expectations to be cared for and begin to ask Jesus, "Will you take care of me, so I am free to minister to other people?"

I have been reading a little novel called *Stepping Heavenward*.[2] It is a collection of journal entries from the time the protagonist was a sixteen-year-old girl all the way through her life, as she tried to live a godly life. It records her victories and her struggles, her stresses and her joys. As a young woman she fell in love with Jesus and determined to live for him for the rest of her life. After a tumultuous start, she married a doctor in a little Vermont village.

The story tells her journey with Jesus as she faced the stressful circumstances in life and learned to trust Him, rather than trying to meet her own needs and fight for her own rights. She found the freedom to lay down her rights and let Jesus meet the needs of her heart like Elijah did—she took her direction, her provision and her protection from Jesus, and then Jesus met her needs.

> *Power means that we can put someone's needs above our own.*

After she married the young doctor, her husband's mother died, and her father-in-law came home from the funeral with the sister-in-law, a grumpy businesslike woman. The father was a melancholy, sick man, and her husband's sister took over the running of the house. One by one Katy had to give up her hopes for her own mother to come with them, and she struggled to learn how to live out her love relationship with Jesus in human relationships that were not of her choosing and did not please her at all. Martha didn't understand her light spirit, and the father-in-law was gloomy and moody and constantly fretting. Her happy household was overshadowed by personalities she did not prefer and responsibilities that she did not expect. In her frustration and pain, Katy began running to Jesus for all these unmet needs, and as she kept coming to Him, Jesus transformed her. At one place she said that although she used to pray because it was her religious duty; now, she prayed because it was the love time of her heart.

Are there any situations in your life that are not to your liking?

Are there any places in your life that you wish were not there?

Are there any circumstances in your life you wish desperately you could change?

Is there pain so deep in your life you think you will die?

I believe those are love presents from Jesus to you and to me that we should receive. Sometimes our gifts from Him come not as beautiful designer gifts but as lumpy brown parcels, but if we receive them from Him, we will find the sweetness of getting to know God Himself. When everything is going well, we act just like Obadiah. We try to do it by ourselves, but when there is severe famine, God can begin to get our attention, and we can begin a love adventure with Him in which He meets the deepest needs of our hearts. That is exactly what happened in *Stepping Heavenward*: Katy became the beloved of the Lord Jesus. Through all those difficult and stressful relationships, God transformed her for her own good and for his glory. The sister-in-law, Martha, became an instrument of blessing. The grumpy daddy loved Katy more than anyone in the world. He refused to leave her until he went to heaven. God moved into her marriage in ways she could never imagine. Jesus transformed her circumstances as she lived out of the love relationship with Him.

> *Sometimes our gifts from Him come not as beautiful designer gifts but as lumpy brown parcels.*

That is also what happens when we allow God to be absolute Lord in our lives, and we stop looking to everyone else to meet our needs and begin to look to Jesus as the lover of our soul no matter the pain in our lives. God can begin to work in the physical circumstances of our lives and make provision for our needs to be met.

The End of the Story

Elijah's dramatic story does not end on top of Mount Carmel. At the end of this chapter, Ahab went to eat and drink, and Elijah went up to pray. One thought of himself; one thought of the nation. Elijah prevailed in prayer for the famine to be broken. As Elijah knelt with his head between his knees, he prayed, "God, it is time for you to come and the famine be broken." Unlike the fire, God did not answer in an instant, so as Elijah prayed, he sent his servant to check for rain:

"Go up now, look toward the sea." So, he went up and looked, and said, "There is nothing." And seven times he said, "Go again."

Then it came to pass the seventh time, that he said, "There is a cloud as small as a man's hand, rising out of the sea!"

So, he said, "Go up, say to Ahab, 'Prepare your chariot, and go down before the rain stops you.'"

Now it happened in the meantime that the sky became black with clouds and wind, and there was a heavy rain. So, Ahab rode away and went to Jezreel. Then the hand of the Lord came upon Elijah; and he girded up his loins and ran ahead of Ahab to the entrance of Jezreel (18:41-45).

God wants to bring revival to His people. He wants to come again in power and in glory as He did on Mount Carmel and in the flooding rain that came after the victory, but God must have one whose heart is clean and undivided. If He has one such heart that is willing to bear a nation, prove God's power, and prevail in prayer, then the revival will begin, and God can accomplish His purposes in an entire nation. Before any of that can happen, our hearts must be single and undivided. He must have first place. I cannot be seeking to use God or use other people to meet my own needs. There

If He has one such heart that is willing to bear a nation, prove God's power, and prevail in prayer, then the revival will begin.

must be a willingness to live in total dependence on Him, awaiting His direction, receiving His provision, honoring His name. The reason that the Western church is so ineffectual is simply because we have divided hearts. We have never settled the issue of who is Lord; we are afraid to say a wholehearted "yes" to the eternal God, so we live our lives half in and half out—wretched, miserable, fearful, and neurotic.

God says, "That is not my plan for you. My plan for you is that you would know love and laughter from me. You would trust me even in the darkest famine to provide for you and give you direction." His care comes when we take the pain he sends in our lives and we embrace Him in that pain, holding on to Him until He does what He needs to do. When He has accomplished that, then he can begin to end the severe famine in our society and in our world. God says, "I can't change the famine until you give me permission to transform you."

A friend told me a story of an African church that was taking an offering. Often in Africa, offerings come in forms other than money: produce or livestock or crops, so baskets are set out to receive the offering. All the church members filed forward, each with something to bring for the basket except for one man. The only thing he had in his hands was an enormous woven basket, much bigger than the basket for the offering. He brought it to the front of the church and put it on the ground. The preacher said, "What are you doing?" Calmly, the man replied, "I have nothing else to bring, so I bring myself." And he promptly climbed into the basket.

Are we willing to bring to Christ our whole lives and our whole selves—all of us for all of Him?

It is not an even exchange; in fact, it is a ridiculous exchange on His part. All the eternal God for weak and wimpy me? He offers Himself, and we can give ourselves to Him. This is the beginning of a beautiful love adventure with Jesus.

At one point in my life, I found myself in a deep dark night of the soul, when God had seemed to pull the rug out from under my feet; everything was chaotic and confusing, and I wondered where God was. I had loved God, served Him, given Him every part of my life, and yet it seemed like He had failed me quite seriously. I did not understand the circumstances in my life, and they were more painful than I could have imagined. My husband and I went to a retreat in North Carolina; it was a retreat for mostly Christian workers, and while I was there, someone I respected came up to me and said, "Beth, you need to meet Connie. She loves Jesus better than anyone I have ever met."

He offers Himself, and we can give ourselves to Him. This is the beginning of a beautiful love adventure with Jesus.

I looked at her, and she seemed like a normal woman.

I said, "What does she do?"

"Well, she is a homemaker. She has three boys."

I said, "Oh"...but I thought, "I don't want to get to know that woman at all, especially in my condition."

I watched her all night. She seemed friendly, but I surely did not want to have anything to do with her. I thought she had it all together, and I had nothing together. Then next morning I was late for breakfast. I came in, and there was only one seat left in that whole dining room. Of course, it was by that woman. I remember standing in that door and saying, "Jesus, why? What will I ever talk about to someone who knows you better than anyone in the whole world? I don't even know what to say to someone like that."

I sat down next to her. We began to talk about children and family life, but the sweetness of Jesus was so real in her life that I found myself in my incredible pain just beginning to sob—not nice little polite cries, but heaving, racking sobs. Everybody was astounded. I was astounded, and poor Al was humiliated. We had to move ourselves out to the porch. I looked at her and I said, "Connie, how do you know Jesus like you do?"

She laughed and said, "One day I was doing the laundry." Don't you love how Jesus transforms our ordinary moments? "We have a landing at my house, and I went up the stairs to the landing, and Jesus was there. It wasn't a vision. I didn't see a dream. It was just his presence. And he spoke to my heart.

'Connie, I have many workers for me; but I have very few lovers of me. Will you ever love me just for who I am, not for what I can do for you, like bless you, use you, help you—even save you? But would you love me for who I am? Just Jesus.'

I put down my laundry basket, and I sat on the stairs and I said, 'Jesus, you have made me just like yourself because there is something in my soul that hungers to be loved just for who I am, not for what I can do, or who I belong to or how smart I am, or if we have money or not, but just because I am Connie.'"

And she said, "I sat there and thought, 'Jesus, yes. I will say yes to you. I will give you *all of me for all of you.*' Do you know, the sweetness of his presence just came and entered my heart? *All of Connie for all of Jesus.*"

Shyly she said, "The only thing I could compare it to was like the consummation of my vows on my wedding night."

"The sweetness was so sweet, I didn't know if I could stand it." She said, "Finally, I had to tell him, 'Jesus, you will have to draw back a little or I will die from the joy.'" She said that in His love, He did. I looked at her and said, "Connie, how do I get there? What do I do?"

Connie laughed and said, "Beth, it is not anything you do. It is a gift given. It is Jesus himself, enveloping, controlling, and consuming the love of your heart. It is a relationship. It is Jesus. Jesus, Jesus, Jesus. In the deepest recesses of who you are, there is Jesus. You enter a love relationship where it is not your will but only his will. Where it is not your words but his words and seeking to make his words your words. Where you become his, and he becomes yours. You stop trying to control and look out for yourself. You trust yourself to Him to take care of you."

She prayed with me that day, but the closeness of her relationship with Jesus was such that it was like Betsy in *The Hiding Place* where all her life seemed to be a prayer. She simply lived in his presence.

> *It is a gift given. It is Jesus himself, enveloping, controlling, and consuming the love of your heart. It is a relationship.*

This is All of Me for All of Jesus! It was true for Elijah, it was true for Connie and it can be true for you and for me today!

I think Jesus is saying,

"Are there any out there who will love me for who I am?

Anyone who will enter a relationship with me not for what you can get but because of who I am?

Anyone who will begin a love adventure with me and ask me to repair the altars of your soul today?"

We can become one who says, Jesus, I trust you to meet every need in my heart.

This life of love is a life in which every known sin is covered and cleansed with His precious blood. And then He teaches us how to work that out in relationships. We can become not one who fights for our own rights, but one who says, "Jesus, I trust you to meet every need in my heart." We can live in a moment-by-moment relationship of love with Jesus Christ.

Personal Reflection

Elijah had an undivided heart. What is your heart like? Are you willing for the difficult places?

Obadiah had a fearful heart. Are you motivated by fear? Do your actions change depending on your circumstances? Take some time with the Lord to ask Him about your motivations.

Ahab had a selfish heart. He was willing to accommodate anything if he got what he wanted. Ask God to clean your heart so you are turned to Him and not to your own self-interest. Self-interest only destroys.

Do you know what it means to give all of you for all of Jesus? To be more than simply a worker for Jesus but one who is filled with His Holy Spirit, living in a love relationship with Him? Take some time to talk to Him about His invitation to this life of exchange that Connie and Elijah knew.

Notes

Notes

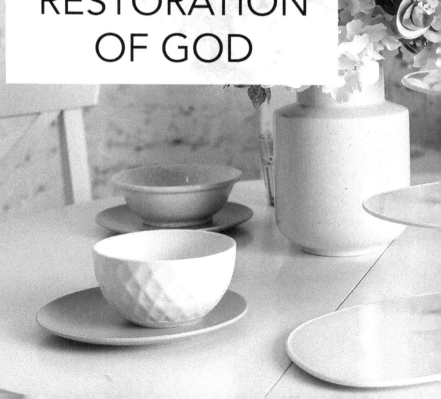

CHAPTER
3

THE
RESTORATION
OF GOD

I love the nineteenth chapter of 1 Kings. For any soldier in the battle who is weary and overwhelmed, this chapter explains the gracious and loving concern of God Himself. Anyone who has known the discouragement that can come after a great spiritual victory understands the lovingkindness of God in chapter 19. Chapter 18 is full of victory and celebration; there is the confrontation between the prophets of Baal and the one prophet of Yahweh. Yahweh wins triumphantly, the false prophets are destroyed, and the famine comes to an end in a deluge of rain. It is a chapter of hallelujahs! Chapter 19 begins with a secret conversation between Ahab and Jezebel, a vicious threat against Elijah's life, and a weary prophet running for his life.

> *And Ahab told Jezebel all that Elijah had done, also how he had executed all the prophets with the sword. Then Jezebel sent a messenger to Elijah, saying, "So let the gods do to me, and more also, if I do not make your life as the life of one of them by tomorrow about this time." And when he saw that, he arose and ran for his life, and went to Beersheba, which belongs to Judah, and left his servant there.*

> *But he himself went a day's journey into the wilderness and came and sat down under a broom tree. And he prayed that he might die, and said, "It is enough! Now, Yahweh, take my life, for I am no better than my fathers!"*

Then as he lay and slept under a broom tree, suddenly an angel touched him and said to him, "Arise and eat."

Then he looked, and there by his head was a cake baked on coals and a jar of water. So, he ate and drank, and lay down again. And the angel of the Yahweh came back a second time, and touched him, and said, "Arise and eat, because the journey is too great for you." So, he arose, and ate and drank; and he went in the strength of that food forty days and forty nights as far as Horeb, the mountain of God (1 Kings 19:1-8).

Perhaps the greatest confrontation in the Old Testament between evil and the God of Israel occurs at Mount Carmel and is recorded in 1 Kings 18. Elijah's challenge to Ahab and the prophets of Baal was a direct assault on the evil which had permeated the people of God, and Elijah had done it without any human aid. No one stood with him (except God Himself) as he confronted the prophets of Baal; in fact, it says that the "people of God didn't answer a word." They just stood by, willing to let the pieces fall where they would. Only at the very end of the chapter, when God had broken through into space and time, did they rally and destroy the prophets of Baal. Elijah alone was willing to say an unqualified and wholehearted "yes" to Yahweh. God came and consumed the sacrifice and the altar; He proved Himself to His own people. In the power of the moment, Elijah and the people quickly

> *Elijah knelt on Mount Carmel and prayed until God answered his cries.*

destroyed the four hundred and fifty false prophets, and then Elijah went to the top of Mount Carmel to pray for an end to the drought. He knelt on Mount Carmel and prayed until God answered his cries.

It was the battle of a lifetime, and afterwards Elijah found himself mentally, physically, emotionally, and spiritually exhausted. Confronting evil has an uncanny way of blindsiding believers. Even when God moves in powerful ways, many times after the victory, the servant of God finds herself in a state of vulnerability.

Elijah had a good reason to fear. After the rain came, Ahab went home and reported to Jezebel about the victory of Yahweh and the deadly consequences for her prophets. Furious and vengeful, she promised to kill Elijah on the very next day, sending him a threatening message of death. Elijah, who withstood the king, four hundred and fifty prophets and an entire nation, trembled at this threat, and in fear he ran away.

> *We are as dependent upon the Spirit of the Living God today as we were yesterday.*

The Tender Mercy of God

In chapter 18, Elijah waited on God, and there is no record of self-initiated activity on his part, but in chapter 19, Elijah fled, and Scripture gives no mention of a Word from the Lord. He was fatigued and afraid. He ran all the way through Israel, down through Judah to the backside of Judah, to Beersheba. Then, he left his servant and traveled another day's journey into the wilderness. Basically, he ran until there was no way Jezebel could ever find him. The courageous prophet of chapter 18 fled in panic and in terror in chapter 19. I love the honesty of Scripture. The power was not in Elijah, and the power is not in us. We are as dependent upon the Spirit of the Living God today as we were yesterday. Sometimes circumstances come that we feel we cannot handle, and we do not wait for God's direction, but we run impulsively and impetuously. Before we know it, we find ourselves on the backside of the desert or even in another land, waiting and wondering how we ended up there. Elijah was not alone in his flight of fear, and he was not alone when he landed in the wilderness; many times, we do exactly the same thing. God Himself came to meet Elijah in the wilderness. He did not come with condemnation and anger, and He will not come that way to us either.

When Elijah finally collapsed under a tree, he began to speak to God. Here is my own interpretation of Elijah's part of that conversation: "God, enough is enough! It would be better just to take my life and get it over. I have done all I can do. I am no better than my fathers; they were killed, and I will be killed. No one can stand against evil and survive." Elijah had stood against evil, and God had an opportunity to prove Himself to the nation of Israel. God had begun the demise of the house of Ahab, which He would continue to accomplish, and He had demolished the worship of Baal in Israel. God had worked powerfully, but Elijah could not see the victory. In his exhaustion, all he could see was that there was a price

> *God did not come to Elijah with condemnation and anger, and He will not come that way to us either.*

on his head, and he was utterly alone. No one had stood with him.

In mercy and grace, God came and met Elijah. He did not give him a lecture. He did not scold him, nor did He remind him of all the wonderful things he had done at Mount Carmel. Instead, God simply put him to sleep, and when Elijah wakened, God sent an angel with food for him. Sometimes despair in the Christian life is simply because we have been on the frontline for God, and we have spent and been spent until our physical resources are exhausted, and there is nothing left.

Rest is a gift, and sometimes when our spiritual condition seems out of whack, we simply need to sleep.

The Great Physician simply says, "Sleep!" Amy Carmichael, the missionary to India's children said that sleep is God's gift. If you fall asleep while you pray, just sleep. *God gives His beloved sleep.* Rest is a gift, and sometimes when our spiritual condition seems out of whack, we simply need to sleep.

I remember one time I had two young toddlers with pneumonia. They did not want anyone but their mama. My verse for that season was, "Many are the afflictions of the righteous, but the Lord delivers out of them all" from Psalm 37. I thought I would never live through the constant days and nights of care, and I remember being so tired I could not think straight. In those moments, we need to nestle into the heart of our loving heavenly Father, and we need to sleep at every opportunity He gives us. The devil likes to use exhaustion to discourage the people of God, when all we need to do is recognize our physical need and rest.

In His love, God provided for Elijah's physical needs. He gave him sleep and then food. Under the pressure and intensity of the battle, Elijah had not eaten enough, and so God restored his body with rest and nutrition. Then, God did it all over again. He put him back to sleep, and then he nourished him again. When God fed him the second time, Elijah journeyed in the strength of it for forty days and forty nights, and God led him from Beersheba to Mount Horeb by the Sinai Peninsula. God took Elijah back to the sacred place where He had first met His people on Mount Sinai. Then the real conversation began.

The Voice of God

I love the conversations between Elijah and God because they are so honest. Elijah is certainly not one to waste words or argue with God, but he is completely transparent in his conversing with God. The conversation between the two of them denotes a deep and abiding friendship. 1 Kings 19:9-16 tells the story.

> And there he went into a cave, and spent the night in that place; and behold, the word of the LORD came to him, and He said to him, "What are you doing here, Elijah?"
>
> So he said, "I have been very zealous for the LORD God of hosts; for the children of Israel have forsaken Your covenant, torn down Your altars, and killed Your prophets with the sword. I alone am left; and they seek to take my life."

Then He said, "Go out, and stand on the mountain before the LORD." And behold, the LORD passed by, and a great and strong wind tore into the mountains and broke the rocks in pieces before the LORD, but the LORD was not in the wind; and after the wind an earthquake, but the LORD was not in the earthquake; and after the earthquake a fire, but the LORD was not in the fire; and after the fire a still small voice.

So it was, when Elijah heard it, that he wrapped his face in his mantle and went out and stood in the entrance of the cave. Suddenly a voice came to him, and said, "What are you doing here, Elijah?"

And he said, "I have been very zealous for the LORD God of hosts; because the children of Israel have forsaken Your covenant, torn down Your altars, and killed Your prophets with the sword. I alone am left; and they seek to take my life."

Then the LORD said to him: "Go, return on your way to the Wilderness of Damascus; and when you arrive, anoint Hazael as king over Syria. Also you shall anoint Jehu the son of Nimshi as king over Israel. And Elisha the son of Shaphat of Abel Meholah you shall anoint as prophet in your place."

Elijah was incredibly open with God. He did not say any spiritual mumbo jumbo; he simply expressed the fatigue and distress of his own heart. God was neither offended nor angry when Elijah spewed out his emotion. It is always good to be honest with God;

He made us, so He knows our emotional needs. We can honestly say, "Father, I am overwhelmed. Father, the pressures seem too great. I feel like I am sinking." God did not scold Elijah; instead, he met him with a fresh vision of Himself. He not-so-gently reminded Elijah that He was still in control by showing a display of His power. He had already proven Himself God over the false gods, and now He proved Himself God over the forces of nature. He put on a firework show for Elijah, hiding him carefully and deliberately in the cleft of the rock as the wind tore through the mountains, the ground shook beneath him, and the fire burned up the side of the mountain. He seemed to be saying to Elijah, "It might look like I am not in control, but I am in control, and you are definitely still under my care."

It is always good to be honest with God; He made us, so He knows our emotional needs.

I read a book called *Karen, Karen* by Karen Mains.[3] She was a busy, young preacher's wife with four small children in the inner city of Chicago. She was completely overwhelmed with her responsibilities, and as it so often happens, the church board did not see eye-to-eye with her husband, and many in their congregations were struggling with drug addictions. They were constantly giving away their money, their time, and their energy to help the people God had given to them.

One morning Karen woke up angry. "God, we are doing everything we know to bring the gospel to Chicago. We are being faithful to you, but we don't have any money, we live in a tiny apartment, and we have four children. Everyone I know is going to Florida for the winter, and I am stuck in cold Chicago with more needs than I can manage and more month than money. I do not think it is fair. I do not think you treat your people very well." Her husband came down into the kitchen and quickly backed out and headed to the church. She was left alone with messy dishes and her tears falling into the sink.

When we trust Him and look to Him to meet our daily needs, we find the joy of learning what it means to be cared for by God Himself.

Just then, the doorbell rang, and she went to open it. There was a UPS box, and it was filled with Florida grapefruits and oranges. "Jesus, that makes me even more mad!" she fumed. "I don't want oranges from Florida; I want to go to Florida!" Karen went up to her room, stretched out on her bed and poured out her heart to her heavenly Father. In His loving way, He came and met her, filled her with His presence, and gave her grace and strength to pick up the kitchen towel, finish the dishes and eat an orange, thinking on His sweetness.

How is it that if He comes, even little apartments with needy children and financial stresses can become sacred and precious places, full of life and love and peace?

Being under the care of the eternal God is the privilege of every believer who keeps herself nestled into the heart of God. When we trust Him and look to Him to meet our daily needs, we find the joy of learning what it means to be cared for by God Himself. God spoke to Elijah, not in the wind or earthquake or fire but with a still, small voice. Elijah heard the whisper, came out of the cave, lifted his eyes to heaven, and listened. God responded to Elijah—heart to heart, friend to friend, and he asked him the same question as before.

"Elijah, what are you doing here?"

All over again, Elijah explained his situation, as if God were not quite smart enough to get it the first time, and then God brought His message of hope to Elijah. It is as if He said to Elijah, "You are not a failure; you are not finished. The best is yet to come. I have a way out for you." And then God gave His servant practical instructions.

God gave him help in the fight, instructing him to go and anoint three men, which was the calling of God on these men's lives. Elijah was not alone in this battle against evil, and God wanted him to know that. These men, Hazel and Jehu, would help wipe out the house of Ahab and rid the land of evil. Two of these men would be kings and the third would be Elijah's own helper and successor. God gave him a friend, a prayer partner, an assistant. He provided someone to stand in the gap with Elijah for the nation of Israel, and then He let Elijah know that there were seven thousand more who had been faithful to Yahweh who had not bowed to any other god.

> *We are made for each other, to be completed by and strengthened in the friendship of one another.*

The bravest prophet of Israel could not make it on his own, and neither can we. We are made for each other, to be completed by and strengthened in the friendship of one another. We need each other. As great a man as Elijah was, he needed support and fellowship of other believers, and God knew it. Elisha became God's answer to Elijah's aloneness; he strengthened Elijah's hand just by coming alongside him.

This encounter between God and Elijah is one of the most dramatic and personal encounters in all the Old Testament. Into Elijah's fear and anxiety, depression and distress, God came with love, with protection, with nourishment, with rest, with His own voice, with reinforcements, and with a plan. God met Elijah in the desperation of his own soul, and He administered strength for the journey. Sometimes God asks His people to pull away for a season to let the angel of the Yahweh feed and minister, speak and direct. This is God's restoration process, and He knows it is needed by all those who love Him and live for Him. He restores! He renews! He refreshes!

He Restores!

He Renews!

He Refreshes!

Provision of God

Elijah arose in the strength of that encounter and he returned to the people of God. Elijah left the mountain and the wilderness, and he went to anoint two kings and find Elisha. When God confronts us and gives us instructions about the next step, He also gives strength to walk into it with purpose and courage:

So, he departed from there, and found Elisha, the son of Shaphat, who was plowing with twelve yokes of oxen before him, and he was with the twelfth. Then Elijah passed by him and threw his mantle on him. And he left the oxen and ran after Elijah, and said, "Please let me kiss my father and my mother, and then I will follow you."

And he said to him, "Go back again, for what have I done to you?"

So, Elisha turned back from him, and took a yoke of oxen and slaughtered them and boiled their flesh, using the oxen's equipment, and he gave it to the people, and they ate. Then he arose and followed Elijah and became his servant (19:19-21).

The impression given of Elisha is that he was a young man, industrious and strong, from a wealthy family even in this time of famine. He was leading a yoke of oxen, but there were eleven other yokes, so he was part of a large farming operation. Out of the blue, Elijah walked up to him, and without saying a word placed the mantle over his shoulders. Elisha recognized him instantly and understood the calling Elijah was placing on him. He knew both its honor and its severity. Elisha's heart was willing, and he asked this gruff old prophet a simple question, "Can I go and say goodbye to my parents before I follow you?"

> *When God confronts us and gives us instructions about the next step, He also gives strength to walk into it with purpose and courage.*

An Ordinary Day with an Extraordinay Call

For Elisha, this was his hour of decision. Scripture does not indicate that Elisha wanted to be the next prophet of Israel. God simply called him, and he had the choice to leave all and follow or not. This sounded much like Jesus' call for His disciples at the Sea of Galilee where the fishermen were washing their nets and Jesus said, "Come and follow me." A moment in time and space that makes all of human history different. Elisha questioned Elijah, but Elijah had no answers to give. The ball was now in Elisha's court, and he had to determine what God wanted of him. This is how God's call must be for everyone. Our calling cannot rest on anyone other than Jesus; ultimately, we are responsible to Him and to Him alone. We must wait on Him until we know we are following His voice and His call on our lives. We cannot follow other human persons. If we do, it will end in failure and disaster.

Our calling cannot rest on anyone other than Jesus.

Elisha left Elijah and returned home to do one very important thing. He threw a party. He sacrificed his oxen, burned his equipment and then served every one of his fellow workers (and I hope his mom and dad) a goodbye meal. From that moment, God was responsible to meet the needs of Elisha. Elisha chose to leave everything else behind, and he did so in order to become the servant of the prophet. He was not signing up for a place of grandeur but a position of servitude. He agreed to be Elijah's servant, waiting on him, caring for him. We become great in the kingdom of God by washing dishes, making meals, serving

God's people. We know Christ, not through great works, but through the Spirit of Jesus giving us the victory for a hundred loads of laundry, for cleaning up messes, for serving those He brings—whether we like them or not.

Can we serve as a love gift to Jesus?

Can we love Jesus by loving others?

As we learn to be faithful here, God can use us in other situations; he used Elisha to turn an entire people group back to God. It is in the little places, the nitty-gritty of life, that we show whether we are truly His or not.

I read an interesting story about a young woman from China. She came to the United States to go to college and then on to medical school. She was a brilliant woman and doctor, and she returned to school to get a double PhD in biochemistry and microbiology from Rice University. Her heart was in research, and some of her research was used by Nobel Prize winners, but she also was a surgeon. Her husband was from China, and they had a beautiful little boy. This little boy had extraordinary gifts in mathematics, but he could not speak, and he would have spells of furious anger and temper. One day when she got home, the nanny had locked the little boy in the closet because he was so out of control, and the mama knew she had to get help. All her medical

> *It is in the nitty-gritty of life, that we show whether we are truly His or not.*

degrees and academic degrees were not enough to meet the needs of this child. She went from doctor to doctor, and finally the little boy was diagnosed with autism. This was at the very beginning stages of autism research. What she read about autism caused her to despair, and she thought, "What am I going to do with this child of mine? I have no idea how to help him." In her trauma, she remembered a Scripture verse that she had memorized as a child, "Come to Me, all *you* who labor and are **heavy laden**, and I will give you rest" (Matt 11:28). In the car that day, God spoke to her heart and said,

"Will you come to me and let me carry your burdens?

Will you accept your need for me and let me be God in your life?"

In the quiet of her car, she accepted God's invitation for salvation. He led her to a Christian doctor, but the doctor was one hundred miles away, and she would need to bring her son in every single day for therapy.

She couldn't both take her son to the doctor every day and continue performing surgeries every morning. She said, "I sat in the car and watched my career go down the drain, but I knew that I had to do all that I could to help my son."

Jesus whispered to her heart, "Will you trust me even in this, and will you serve this child I have given you? Will you serve me while loving him?" She resigned from her surgical position and kept only her research work. They began to work with that doctor to help her son learn to talk, and one day after ten years, he was playing Scrabble with another doctor, and the doctor put down a made-up word. The boy knew it was wrong, and he said, "NO, NO, NO!" The mama was ecstatic, and that night before he went to bed, he had said the word, "Mom."

When her husband heard him utter "Mom," he said, "I know Jesus is stronger and more powerful than anyone. He has the capacity to heal our son." They continued to work with that son, and God helped him not only survive but thrive. He has degrees in computer science and mathematics. At the end of the story, the magazine reported that he had been to Hong Kong and had been given an opportunity to give his testimony, how Jesus had touched him and made a way for him. And his doctor mother sat proudly next to him.

God asks for a greatness that is bigger than the world's greatness. He asks for success on His terms, not on ours. Success is when we begin to do what God wants us to do, no matter the cost. We get our direction from Him, and we are willing to lay down our lives for Him. When we lay aside our desire to make a name for ourselves, when we lay aside spiritualized ambition and self-love, God can use us. He asked Elijah, "Can I make you a servant to Elijah, my prophet?" We may never get laurels on earth. When Jesus comes again, though, it will be interesting to see those he takes and embraces and says, "Well done!" We desire to be big and flashy and sensational, and God may be asking us today to die to hopes, dreams, and plans for our own lives, so that God-sized dreams can be accomplished in and through us.

> *Success is when we begin to do what God wants us to do, no matter the cost.*

Prayer Challenge

Many times, God's people think,

"What can I do against the evil that threatens our nation, homes and families?"

We sit under the tree and say, 'Woe is me!" or we sit in our homes and say, "Woe is me! I have tried! I have done all I could do, and it amounted to nothing." I believe God has an answer for us, just like He had for Elijah. I think God wants to challenge us to forty days of prayer. Elijah went in the strength of God's food for forty days, and I think God is asking us to make a covenant to pray for revival every day for forty days.

> *God wants us to pray for our communities, our churches, our states, our nation, and even our world.*

He wants us to pray for the three people in our lives who do not know Jesus as their Savior whom God is putting on our hearts. I call them our Three Most Wanted. I also think He wants us to pray for our communities, our churches, our states, our nation, and even our world.

Ask God to place one country of the world on your heart and pray for that nation every single day for the next forty days.

Get a prayer partner and begin to pray together for your families, your children, your marriages, your neighbors.

A friend of mine gave this challenge to her church in Latin America. She challenged the church members to be soul-winning churches. One year, she asked every Christian in that church to win four people to Jesus Christ in the course of the year, pray for them every day, give them a Bible and invite them to attend church. The whole church heard it, and one little boy took it to heart and began to pray seriously for his friend at school. He was invited to this friend's birthday party. He wanted to give his friend a Bible, but his mom tried to discourage it. She was quite sure that a Bible would not be the best present for an elementary-aged child. But her son was determined. "That is what I am supposed to do!" he insisted. They bought the Bible, and the little boy wrote on the card, "Have your mommy and daddy read this to you every day. It will tell you how to know Jesus and how to get to heaven." The little boy signed his name on the inside of the Bible and took it to the party.

Two weeks later, the mother received a call from the mother of the little friend. She said, "Oh, thank you for giving that Bible to my son. We cannot let a day go by without reading the Bible because he wants to go to heaven, and he wants to know Jesus. So, every night my husband and I are reading that Bible to our son, but we have so many questions. We do not understand it. Would you ever be able to tell us what it means because we would like to go to heaven and know Jesus too." The mother, feeling a little ashamed, invited the whole family to church. The next Sunday, with a great victorious smile, the little boy marched into church and sat on his row with his friend, his friend's mom and dad and sister. All four found Jesus!

If God can do it for that child, he can do it for us.

Let's begin to ask God for our three most wanted, and then say, "Would you show me how to reach them now?"

He also wants us to get a prayer partner, just like God gave Elijah a helper in Elisha. He wants to give us someone with whom we can pray and with whom we can stand in the gap for our loved ones. On the day that you pray with your prayer partner, practice some form of self-denial. It does not always have to be food, but it may be. It could be an afternoon coke or a night of television, but ask Jesus what is something that you can give for love of Him. It lets Him know that you are serious: "Jesus, enough is enough! I have prayed for these people for years now, and it is time that they found Jesus! I am fasting and praying so that they can know you and get to heaven." This is the beginning of Revival Praying.

Gypsy Smith once explained how a revival begins, "Go home. Lock yourself in your room, kneel in the middle of the floor and draw a chalk mark all around yourself. Ask Jesus to start the revival inside that circle of chalk. When he has answered your prayer, the revival will be on!" We need to pray, "Oh Jesus, start the revival in me! Then come and touch my family, my community, my church, my state, my nation, and the whole world. The devil has had the people I love long enough! He has had my nation and this world long enough. It is time for you to come!"

I told this story at a retreat, and I gave everyone a piece of chalk and challenged them to go home and start a revival. One little lady took me seriously, and she went home, drew a chalk mark around herself and asked Jesus to start a revival within the circle. Jesus began right away to talk to her about starting a Bible study in her home. She invited her friends, and twelve women showed up. They had precious prayer times, and then one day she gave them all a piece of chalk and shared with them the challenge by Gypsy Smith. They took the chalk but looked unimpressed; she knew that the challenge had not made an impression on them at all. One day while shopping, she saw some hula-hoops, and Jesus whispered to her heart an idea for her Bible study ladies. The next week the ladies were surprised when they met at the church and twelve hula-hoops were in front of the altar. At the end of the prayer time, she said, "If you would like God to start a revival in your life, go and stand in the hula-hoop and invite Him to start the revival in you." The ladies hesitated, but then one by one they went and stood in the circle of the hula hoops, asking Jesus to start the revival in the circle. He did! In fact, the pastor of the church heard what God had done, and he went out and bought the largest hula-hoop he could find. The church had a board with the names of all the prodigals for whom they were praying. He put the hula hoop around all those names, and within two weeks the most lost one on that list had found Jesus. He wrote his mom from prison and said, "I think God is calling me to go to Bible school." Revival in one spread to revival in twelve which spread to revival in a church.

He wants to make us women and men of prayer, and He wants to use us to reach the world for Him.

We can only make a difference for God if our hearts are squeaky clean, and if we are willing to follow Him wherever He leads us. He wants to make us women and men of prayer, and He wants to use us to reach the world for Him. During the ordinariness of life, God wants to come and meet us in prayer, so that we can be a powerhouse for Him wherever He puts us. God is looking for those who will be lovers of Him and workers with Him in prayer.

> *God wants to come and meet us in prayer, so that we can be a powerhouse for Him wherever He puts us.*

Personal Reflection

Do you know the exhaustion that comes from spiritual battle? Have you felt the depression of spirit that comes after a victory is won by the Lord? If so, how has God restored your spirit? Take some time to think of His ways of restoration in your own life.

Do you feel free to be as honest with God as Elijah was when your emotions are discouraged and gloomy?

Like Elisha, are you willing to come alongside another, serving, loving, praying, even if it means you don't get the credit?

Notes

Notes

Notes

CHAPTER
4

SQUEAKY CLEAN
HEARTS

The stories of Elijah and Elisha continue in a very political and dramatic way. Suddenly, the attention pivots from God's care of Elijah to the kings of Israel and Judah. Jehoram, the son of Ahab, had become king of Israel and Jehoshaphat the king of Judah. Jehoshaphat was a good man; his story is given in 2 Chronicles 17-19; he sought the Lord and removed the high places. He had done many good things for the Lord. Jehoram, king of Israel, was an evil man, although not as corrupt as Ahab and Jezebel. He tried to get rid of the worship of Baal, but he continued in the worship of Jeroboam. Jeroboam had started the kingdom of Israel on their downward trek into idolatry when they established the worship of calves in Dan and in Bethel. God had told His people to go to Jerusalem for all worship; the God of Israel did not want shrines all over like the other nations. He wanted one location where the people would all come together to worship a few times a year. King Jehoram tried to make it easier, and so he set up high places and shrines in other parts of Israel so that the people did not have to travel for worship. The people began to worship images of God instead of God Himself, and idolatry flourished in Israel, a breaking of the second Commandment given to Moses. Jeroboam replaced the reality of the presence of God with idols. This unlikely pair joined forces in 2 Kings 3.

Moab had rebelled against the Northern kingdom and refused to pay tribute to them, so Jehoram asked Jehoshaphat to come and fight with Israel against the Moabites. Jehoshaphat controlled

Edom, so when he went to fight with Israel, Edom went as well to help in the fight against Moab. For some reason, which the writer of Kings does not tell us, Jehoshaphat did not seek the counsel of God. He was aware of the evil in Israel, but still he joined forces with Jehoram to help him fight his battles. Instead of inquiring of the Lord, he simply responded to the need of the moment, acting in a way that seemed beneficial to his own interests and the interests of Judah. Jehosophat forgot his first allegiance to God and hastily entered into an alliance that would only bring destruction to his household.

How often the enemy comes as an angel of light! 2 Chronicles 20 tells how Jehoshaphat had fought against Moab previously under the direction of God. He had fought by prayer and by praise, by fasting and by humility. An incredible victory came to him. It is one of the classic triumphs in all of Scripture, but this time Jehoshaphat tried to do it in his own strength, and he did not wait on the Lord. The kings from Judah and Edom headed out, and they immediately ran into trouble; they lost their way in the wilderness and ended up on the backside of the desert with no water for their troops. The kings should have known which way to lead their troops, but sin and disobedience to the known will of God often produce blindness and stupidity.

> *Sin and disobedience to the known will of God often produce blindness and stupidity.*

The king of Israel said, "Alas! For the Lord has called these three kings together to deliver them into the hand of Moab." Although God was not consulted, the king of Israel places all the blame on God. Jehoshaphat, king of Judah, had a little more integrity than that, and he began to regret not asking the Lord for direction:

> And the king of Israel said, "Alas! For the LORD has called these three kings together to deliver them into the hand of Moab."
>
> But Jehoshaphat said, "Is there no prophet of the LORD here, that we may inquire of the LORD by him?"
>
> So one of the servants of the king of Israel answered and said, "Elisha the son of Shaphat is here, who poured water on the hands of Elijah."
>
> And Jehoshaphat said, "The word of the LORD is with him." So the king of Israel and Jehoshaphat and the king of Edom went down to him (2 Kings 3:10-12).

Are there any circumstances in your life in which you find yourself because you did not ask God, and you end up in the backside of the desert, thirsty and without provision, asking, "God, how did I get here?"

And God says, "Well, let me tell you. You did not ask me what to do."

The kings (just like us) begin to ask God for a way out. "God, is there any way you could get me out of this? I sure am thirsty, and I hate to have this be the end of my life. Is there any way you can get me out?"

God, in his compassion, bails out these three kings. When they arrive to inquire of Elisha, there is a forced humility in those three kings simply because of their incredible duress. They go to Elisha. They do not send anyone to bring him to them. Elisha responds with the confidence of a prophet of the Lord.

He says, "What have I to do with you? Go to the prophets of your father and the prophets of your mother...."

> And Elisha said, "As the LORD of hosts lives, before whom I stand, surely were it not that I regard the presence of Jehoshaphat king of Judah, I would not look at you, nor see you (2 Kings 3:14).

Elisha knows the character of Jehoshaphat, and it is that which saves the other two kings. Jehoshaphat was in a place in which he should not have been, allied with men with whom he should not have been involved. Anytime we choose to accommodate evil and sin in our hearts, we will end up on the backside of the desert lost and in need.

Elisha said, "I will have nothing to do with you in your rebellion against God, and if not for something good in Jehoshaphat, I would not even speak to you." If we are to be people of God, people after God's own heart, there has to be something in our hearts that will not accommodate sin or evil or align ourselves with it. In Ephesians 3 and 4, Paul talks about exposing the works of darkness. Christians are not

Anytime we choose to accommodate evil and sin in our hearts, we will end up on the backside of the desert lost and in need.

to participate in them. We need to say, "Jesus, give us your understanding, so we are not enticed and pulled away from you. You know the hearts of men and women; we do not know them. Let us not be a part of evil situations that will bring death and damnation to others."

Elijah asks for a musician and when he plays, the hand of the LORD came upon him. And he said, "Thus says the LORD: Make this valley full of ditches." For thus says the LORD: "You shall not see wind, nor shall you see rain; yet that valley shall be filled with water, so that you, your cattle, and your animals may drink." And this is a simple matter in the sight of the LORD; He will also deliver the Moabites into your hand. Also you shall attack every fortified city and every choice city, and shall cut down every good tree, and stop up every spring of water, and ruin every good piece of land with stones (2 Kings 3:15-19).

There are always consequences when we get out of the will of God and begin to move in the flesh instead of in the spirit.

Unholy Alliances

God answered the prayers of this unlikely and unholy trio. He delivered them from their enemies, but he did it at a cost. There are always consequences when we get out of the will of God and begin to move in the flesh instead of in the spirit. Think back to Abraham. When he got tired of waiting on God, he and Sarah decided to help God out in his will for their lives, and the result was Ishmael. God forgave Abraham, and he ultimately produced Isaac, but the ongoing results of that decision reverberate even today. There are consequences for not living in the Spirit and walking in the Spirit day by day and moment by moment. God is not mean or cruel; God is trying to protect us and keep us from pain and consequences of sin that he does not want us to have to bear.

A leanness comes to our souls when you and I begin to do things in our own strength and get things in our own way.

The victory came to the three kings, but it came at a great price. When Moab sensed that they were about to be defeated, the king of Moab took his son, his firstborn son, the one that would reign in his place, and he offered him as a living human sacrifice on the wall of the city. The Israelites and men of Judah were so horrified by the depth and depravity of that kind of "worship" they all disbanded and went home.

Who was participating in this battle of complete compromise and defeated victory? Good King Jehoshaphat. He should not have been. Yes, God came through, but a leanness comes to our souls when you and I begin to do things in our own strength and get things in our own way. When we manipulate, or we try to control circumstances instead of waiting for God to bring them to us, we pay the price for our lack of faith. God gave them the victory, but He did it in His way. There was no way any of the three kings could take credit for this win. It was all God's work, and there was not even a shot fired by Judah.

Are you in any unholy alliances today?

Is there anything in your life that is not right?

Can you be bought and sold in your Christian walk?

Is the bottom line your own security?

Are you coming to the place where you say, "Jesus, I believe you and you alone are the ultimate security in my life, and I believe that the thing I need more than anything else is an obedient heart that says 'yes' to the will of God no matter what it costs me"?

Isobel Kuhn, a missionary to China, wrote a book entitled *Second Mile People.*[4] As a college girl, Isobel was an agnostic and did not believe in God. Then God met her, and she came into a relationship with Jesus Christ and began to walk with him. God led her to Moody Bible Institute and then filled her with His Spirit. Through a series of different circumstances God led her to the Lisu people in the interior of China on the Burmese border. She was a woman with Jesus as the passion of her soul. She wrote this book called *Second Mile People* about six people that influenced her as a believer that was never published during her lifetime; it was found in a dresser drawer after she died of cancer.

In this book Isobel tells the story of Dorothy, a girl who influenced her when she was just starting her life with Christ. She said there was such a surrender and radiance in Dorothy's life that she felt drawn to her instantly. Her combination of sparkling joy and love for

Christ was an irresistible combination to Isobel's heart. At a Bible conference, Dorothy asked Isobel to go with her on a walk. They laughed and talked as they walked. But afterward, Dorothy felt that she had failed because she did not deal with Isobel about spiritual matters. She sensed that Isobel's heart was only partially surrendered. Isobel said later that although Dorothy didn't speak to her that day of Jesus and full surrender, there was something so deep in her life, and the passion of her soul for God was so real that even though she never spoke the words at that moment directly to Isobel, she knew that Dorothy's life was indwelt by the whole presence of the Eternal God and her heart grew hungry.

Dorothy called her one day and asked her to come help her pack as she prepared to go to China as a missionary. Isobel could not believe that her sweet Dorothy would be a missionary! As they worked, Isobel began to ask questions about Dorothy's willingness to leave all to follow Jesus to the ends of the earth. Dorothy sat down on the side of the bed and began to explain to Isobel what full surrender meant and that the sweetness of Jesus' presence and living reality was so dear that she would follow Him to the ends of the globe if she could keep the sweetness of the presence of God in her life. Isobel could not understand all the words that Dorothy spoke, but her heart spoke to Isobel's heart through the Holy Spirit who began to draw Isobel to Himself.

Dorothy was a *potato chip* Christian. A life so salty with His presence that other people just thirsted for more of Him.

There is no way we can live like that unless we are squeaky clean. The bottom line is that Jesus is our ultimate security, and we would rather die than disobey Him or to move out in our own fleshly, natural way.

The day came when Dorothy came back from China. When she came back she brought a diamond ring from Isobel's fiancé, John Kuhn, who was also a missionary in China. Their hearts had been knit before, but they were really knit now. As Isobel got that diamond from her beloved on the other side of the globe, this beautiful smiling young woman shared in her joy. Once again, Isobel's heart was drawn, and she knew that she wanted to know Jesus like Dorothy did. Isobel went to China and married John. God was working in their lives and in their ministry. One day Isobel received the news that Dorothy had died of typhoid fever in the middle of China. Dorothy's last question to her caregiver and friend was simply, "Are you willing even for this?" When Isobel heard her last words, they resonated over and over in her mind.

"Am I willing even for this, Jesus so that your name might be glorified, so that the lost might find you and so that I might know you not just know about you?"

Radical Christianity

I would like to talk to you today about radical Christianity. Radical Christianity means that the bottom line in my life is not security, prestige, money or power, but Jesus Christ.

As we begin to allow Him to be the center of our lives, He transforms us to live in freedom and joy. These are the places where we see what matters to us the most, and if in our lives symbols of His presence (church, religious activity, human effort) have replaced the reality of the eternal presence of God.

I remember talking to a woman who was in her 70s who had walked with God and was walking with him still, with a passion and a fire like an Elijah or Elisha. I asked, "Where did it all begin?" She said, "It began when I found him, and He filled me with his Holy Spirit. I remember I was living at home, and my folks watched TV every night, and suddenly, I could not watch it anymore at night. In my heart I began to be drawn up to my bedroom and God began to teach me his word and teach me how to pray."

God wants to get ahold of our choices and teach us to make God choices. When we begin to put God first and seek Him first, He begins to work in the other areas of our lives. There comes an incredible creativity, and so instead of becoming fanatical and narrow-minded, we become open—free in every area of our lives. God begins to move because the focus of our life is centered on the One that matters. Out of that kind of love relationship with Jesus Christ, creativity flows and overflows into every single area of our lives.

It is only as we begin to meet Him and there begins to be transformed choices in the little nitty-gritty of life, that we find the freedom and joy of loving Him.

Jesus can do it today because He cares about every area of our lives. Sometimes the devil whispers in our ear, "You don't want to be fanatical. You really need to be well-rounded instead of sold-out to Jesus Christ." If we listen, we begin to hesitate. What will it mean if we give ourselves to Jesus 100%? The ultimate reality is who we are in relationship to Jesus Christ.

Will I give Him all of me or will I hold back to protect or promote myself?

Jesus is looking for some who are willing to fall in love with Jesus and let Him have all of life without worrying about what anyone else thinks or says.

Jehoshaphat made one error: he did not inquire of the Lord. God had blessed him, and he was not as dependent on God's help as he had been. He became wealthy, and perhaps he was pleased when Ahab came to him. He did not inquire of God, and therefore he entered into a working relationship with a man that had sold himself to do evil. The fruits of that were deadly, not only to the king of the Moabite's family but also to the Jehoshaphat's own family. His son, Jehoshaphat's precious firstborn son, Jehoram, married Ahab's granddaughter. Her name was Athaliah. When Jehoshaphat died, do you know what happened? Jehoshaphat left a lovely inheritance for each of his sons. He left them lands and gold. He cared for all six of his sons, but he made his firstborn, Jehoram, king. Jehoshaphat was barely dead in the grave when Jehoram murdered every single one of his brothers, Jehoshaphat's sons. Jehoshaphat had no idea that in the little bit of time he courted evil, his son would ally himself with Ahab's granddaughter who would be the First Lady of Judah and that Ahab's granddaughter would incite Jehoram (it didn't take much) to murder all the royal family. Evil alliances produce evil—generations of evil.

> *Jesus is looking for some who are willing to simply fall in love with Jesus.*

Results of Our God-Choices

Jerhoram died a horrible death, and no one mourned for him. They were glad he was gone. He was not even buried with the other kings. His youngest son, Ahaziah, became king. When Ahaziah died, his mother, Athaliah became queen. She murdered every one of her grandchildren to make room for her to be the undisputed queen of Judah. Evil reproduced itself in quick and deadly ways. It looked like the devil was going to wipe out the whole family of David, except for two faithful God-fearers who rescued baby Joash from the queen's evil anger. The priest and the nurse took little Joash and hid him in the temple for seven years. Then, they called together the people of Judah and declared Joash to be the legitimate king of Judah.

God is calling us to root out sin; He wants to give us hearts that are squeaky clean.

It was only one time that Jehoshaphat forgot to inquire of God and courted sin. Only one time, but the repercussions went on generation after generation. God is not mean when He says to us "walk before me and be blameless" (Genesis 17:1), because He knows the consequences of sin are lethal. They are lethal, not only here but for all of eternity. The choices you and I make today have consequences for this generation, the next generation, and the generations to come.

God is calling us to root out sin; He wants to give us hearts that are squeaky clean. Let God make you like Dorothy, so that there is nothing between you and Him. Not only will it bring blessing in your life now and the sweetness of His presence, but it will bring blessing, honor, and peace to your children, your grandchildren, and your great grandchildren—all the way to the thousandth generation.

This week I re-read part of the book *Hudson Taylor's Spiritual Secret.*[5] There was a couple that lived in England. They began to pray for the country of China. They said, "Jesus if you would give us a son, we give that son to you and we give you that son to go to China." God gave them a son, and they never told the son of their promise, but they prayed about it. James Hudson Taylor grew up in their home, and it was a godly home. They kept praying for their boy, but he was indifferent to the things of God. When he was a teenager, he decided he did not want to follow God, and he entered a path of agnosticism. His mother began to pray. His sister began to pray. Later they found in her diary that his sister had covenanted to pray every single day until her brother found God. The mother was called away for two weeks of holiday. She was visiting family, and one day at noon she felt an incredible burden for this 17-year-old son. She left the company and went up to her room, put the key in the lock and she said, "Jesus, I am not going to let go until you give me the soul of my son, the son that I have given you since before his birth." She prayed hour after hour in that little bedroom. God's presence came, and she was flooded

> *When there is nothing between you and God, it will bring blessing in your life and the sweetness of His presence.*

with joy. She knew Jesus Christ had heard her mother's heart cry for that boy.

She was right. Hudson was home one dreary afternoon. Nobody else was there, and he went into the library to look for something to read, and he found a tract and thought he would just read the story part. As he read, the Spirit of Jesus dealt with his heart, and Hudson Taylor found God. When his mother came home, he rushed out to tell her his good news, but she exclaimed, "I already know! Jesus told me two weeks ago that you know him." God began to stir this teenager's heart for the country of China, and the burden would not go away. He began to say, "God, I'll be all yours for China." He started preparing to be a missionary. He lowered his standard of living. He began to live by faith. He prayed, "If I get to China, I need to know how to trust you to meet my needs, so could you begin to meet my needs here in England before I go?" So, he came up with a motto that is still Overseas Missionary Fellowship's motto today: *Trust God to move people and things by prayer alone.*

Hudson was a medical student, and he worked for a doctor who was very good man, but he would forget to pay him at times. He told Hudson, "If I forget, just tell me when your pay is due." Hudson began to make it a matter of deep prayer. He said, "God, when he forgets I am not going to remind him. I am going to let you remind him. I'm going to see if you can move a man's heart by prayer." The test came. He began to run out of money, and as he got closer to the end of the month, he sought the Lord and began to pray. "Lord, you know, it's the end of the month, and I don't have any funds coming in. I can't remind my employer. You're going to have to remind him." The Friday before he needed to pay his landlady, he had no money. Then the doctor came and said, "Isn't it about time for me to pay you?" It was almost the last Friday of the month, and Hudson had been praying all week. His heart soared, and he said, "Well, yes, it is."

Then the doctor said, "I'm so sorry. I don't have any bank notes to pay you now. I'll just pay you Monday." Hudson had no food left, and he needed to pay his landlady. His heart sank, and he walked home very sadly.

Trust God to move people and things by prayer alone.

At home, he laid his burdens before the Lord and said, "Lord, I am still looking to you. You know the rent is due. You know there is no money. You know I am still looking to you!" In spite of these dire circumstances, joy came into his heart. That night he went back to the surgery center. He had forgotten something, and as he was finishing up his work in the surgery center he heard the gate open and somebody coming. It was the doctor.

"Do you know what?" asked the doctor. He was laughing. "I had the funniest experience. One of the richest patients just paid his whole bill, right now in the middle of the night. He said he just couldn't settle tonight until he paid me. I just came by to log it. That's most unusual. Why didn't he wait until Monday? I don't need it tonight."

Hudson stood there watching, his heart flip-flopping up and down as he looked at the doctor who logged it in, and then as he got ready to go he handed Hudson something. "Now Hudson, here's part of your salary. I will give you the rest Monday. This should tide you over until then."

Hudson could not even look at the doctor as he walked out because he said he knew in his heart as he held those banknotes there would be enough for food and enough for the landlady. Hudson had begun to trust God for his needs in England, and God had provided in a precious way. Hudson knew he could trust the living God to meet his needs in China too. He walked home that night in awe of how God had provided for him.

Do we know Him like that?

Are there any needs in your life and my life?

Are we trying to meet them in our own strength?

Are we going to the world to get our solutions?

Are we making alliances with Ahab and Jezebel and Jehoram? Do we say, "Surely, God understands? We've got to eat, don't we? We've got to live. Surely He understands."

God says, "No. No. Don't go that way. Don't try to do it in your own strength. That is the reason I am here. I am the God that can bring springs in a desert without wind or rain. I am the God that can deliver you from the Moabites, so they see blood instead of water. I am the God that can move mountains to take care of you, but I allow you to go through these circumstances because I want to see what is in your heart. Do you love me? Do you really love me? Are you just wanting to use and manipulate me like the rest of the world?"

> *God can bring springs in a desert without wind or rain.*

"Is there anyone there that loves me for who I am and is willing to say, 'Jesus Christ, I throw myself into your arms. I stake my life, my security, on you'?"

It will be out of that kind of passionate devotion to Jesus Christ that rivers of living water will flow. Do you know what God did with that one man, birthed out of the prayers of that godly couple? He changed the course of Christian history for the people of China.

What does God want to do with you and me?

God wants to make us people after God's own heart, squeaky clean. He wants to set us free, set us free with a passion for Jesus Christ so that the blessing of God can be on our children and our grandchildren and great-grandchildren.

> *Every person's salvation begins in someone else's obedience.*
> *–Dennis Kinlaw*

Jesus Christ loves us so much. He is utterly trustworthy, and He has your best interest at heart—mine, too. He wants to get you and me into this perfect center of a relationship with Him and the perfect center of His will so that we begin to see the evidence of His presence in our lives, relationships, homes, marriages, workplaces, and future.

Do you trust Him?

Personal Reflection

Are there any unholy alliances in your life? Any people that you have partnered with or allowed to influence you that lead you away from the presence and promises of God? Take some time to pray through the different areas and relationships in your life.

After you have inquired of the Lord, ask Him specifically how to begin to make right what has become unholy in your life? He will give you a plan if you wait on Him for each direction and each step.

The possibilities of your family depend on your obedience to what God shows you. Get out a picture of your family and ask Jesus to cleanse your heart so that He can work in the lives of those you love.

Notes

Notes

Notes

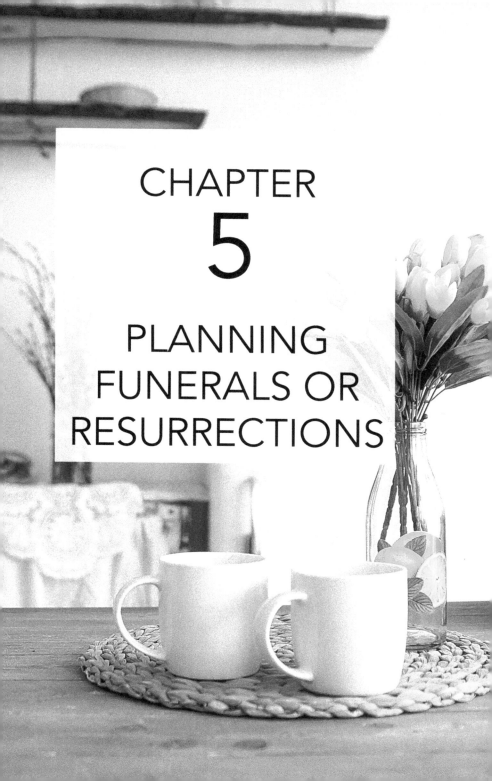

CHAPTER
5

PLANNING
FUNERALS OR
RESURRECTIONS

CHAPTER 5 — PLANNING FUNERALS OR RESURRECTIONS

For many years, 2 Kings 4 has been one of my favorite passages of Scripture. In this chapter, we find two different women in severely difficult situations. The first woman is a widow of one of the prophets of the Lord. She comes to see Elisha in desperation and said,

> *"Your servant, my husband, is dead and you know that your servant feared the Lord. The creditor is coming to take away my two sons to be his slaves."*
>
> *Elijah replied, "What should I do for you? Tell me what you have in your house?"*
>
> *She answered, "Your maidservant has nothing in the house at all but a jar of oil."*
>
> *Then he said, "Go, borrow vessels from everywhere, from all your neighbors' empty vessels. Do not just gather a few, and when you have come in, you shall shut the door behind you and your sons. Then pour in oil to all those vessels. Set aside the full ones."*
>
> *She went from him and she shut the door behind her and her sons who brought her vessels, and she poured it out. Now it came to pass when the vessels were full that she said to her sons, "Bring me another vessel." And they said, "There are no more vessels." Then the oil ceased, and she came and told the man of God.*

Go, sell the oil and pay your debt. You and your sons live on the rest (2 Kings 4:1-7).

This chapter in God's Holy Word is about women and families. Up to this point in the story of Elijah and Elisha, we have been talking about international intrigue and national crises. In between Israel and Judah, God has worked in the lives of prophets, kings, and nations. Then, suddenly waltzing across the pages of Scripture we have two women with burdens on their hearts for their sons. In the last chapter, the king of Moab sacrificed his son and heir; in this chapter two women plead with the prophet about

> *God has a special place in His heart for women in desperate situations.*

the future of their sons. God is incredibly interested and involved in international affairs, in governors and kings, but He is even more concerned about individual people. He has a special place in His heart for women in desperate situations. Both of the women in 2 Kings 4 find in the Lord the answer to their own desperate need. One woman is a widow with two sons. She owes money, and the creditor will take her sons to pay the debt if she does not pay him. The other woman has a husband and a son given to her by God. Her son dies, and she runs to the prophet to get God's answer. Both courageous women cope with their needs by seeking God in the difficult places of life.

The Creditor is Coming

The first story is about the wife of one of Elisha's junior prophets. This couple had faithfully served the Lord, and he died. She found herself unable to pay her bills, and in that day if you did not pay your bills, the creditor could take your children and enslave them. This woman, who had already known extreme suffering in the loss of her husband, went to the prophet of the Lord to try and prevent the enemy from taking her two sons. She looked to the God of Israel to meet her need.

> *When we come to Him in prayer, He desires that we express to Him our need and our request.*

I love Elisha's answer. He listened, and then he looked at her and said, "What can I do for you?" The Holy Spirit gives his men and women a tenderness of spirit and a sensitivity to others in pain. Oftentimes people simply need the catharsis of being able to share painful circumstances with another listening ear. God can use that in a tremendous way to bring healing to any human heart. This is also what Jesus said to many who came to Him for healing, even when it seemed obvious. "What do you want me to do for you?" When we come to Him in prayer, He desires that we express to Him our need and our request.

Then Elisha asks, "What do you have in your house?" This woman was destitute; all she had was a small pot of oil, two sons, and faith in the living God. God wants each one of us to come to the place where we recognize our need for Him. He wants to get us to the place where we ask Him for His help, where we come to Him in humility and say, "Jesus, this is all I have. I cannot meet the needs of my own heart nor the needs of those around me. The creditor is coming for my children, and I am desperate for them." When we recognize that we are destitute in and of ourselves to meet the need in our own strength, we have the freedom to come to God Himself and ask Him to work for us.

Elisha told this woman to go and borrow jars from her neighbors. God likes to meet our needs using the resources of other people. God wanted this widow to ask in faith and vulnerability from her neighbors. She had to walk in obedience and let the community in which she lived know that she had a need. Her community responded with love, and the boys brought jugs and bottles from every neighbor. Their mama continued to obey the prophet's instructions. She went into her house with her boys, who had front row seats for the miracle of God, and she began to pour oil from her own vessel into the jars of her friends. The oil continued to flow until every vessel was full. She turned to look at the boys expectantly, but there were no more jugs to be found.

When we recognize that we are destitute in and of ourselves to meet the need in our own strength, we have the freedom to come to God Himself and ask Him to work for us.

I love her simplicity. She went back to Elisha and says, "Now, what do I do?" He responded, "Sell what you have, pay your creditor and live on the rest." She obeyed, and her sons were saved. The faith and determination of a mother in a time of desperation proved all God needed to save her sons.

Is there a need in our lives today? In our financial lives? Emotional lives? In the lives of our children?

Does it seem like the enemy of your soul is making a bid for the lives of your children?

He does seem to be after our children through addictions, distractions and temptations, like our nation has never seen before. The creditor is coming to our door and saying, "I want your children!"

We have to seek God's face every day and be willing to pay the price so that our children will have the privilege of knowing Jesus Christ.

Here is a picture of a determined mama who said, "Oh no! I am going to stand in the gap for those two boys. The enemy cannot have my sons. My only hope is to go to God Himself, and I will go, and I will do exactly what He tells me to do." In her destitution, she did not look anywhere else except to the living God. She looked to Him, and He gave her a plan for the salvation of her sons.

Our nation is living in an age when a child is considered an inconvenience. We want to do our own thing, and we do not want to be burdened with the cares of children. Our children are fed on electronics from morning to night, and many have no one to pray for them, love them, guide them, and invest in them. We need some mothers, fathers, grandmothers, grandfathers, aunts and uncles who will stand up and say to the creditor of our children's souls, "I will not let that child go!"

We must be on our knees. We cannot do it all at once; we have to seek God's face every day and be willing to pay the price so that our children will have the privilege of knowing Jesus Christ. This is a daily carrying in our being the ones that God has entrusted to us, whether they are our own flesh and blood or the neighborhood children down the street. God is crying out to His people today. The biggest business in the world is to be part of the family that carries the next generation in our hearts.

I went to a retreat in New York, and as we sat around the table I asked each woman how she had met Jesus. Almost everyone said, "I had a neighbor lady who picked me up and took me to church," or "I had a neighbor who invited me to Good News Club or to a Christian camp." A generation of women showed Jesus' love and reached out to the little ones around them.

Are we too busy to invest in the next generation?

He wants to open our eyes and protect our children from the creditor knocking at the door.

As we raise our children and our grandchildren and our neighbor children for God, He wants to move in and capture their hearts. As our families meet difficult circumstances— emotional, financial, or psychological—and as the

The enemy does not want Christian homes to prosper.

enemy of our souls comes to destroy our families, we must get on our faces before God, standing in the gap for our children. We need to cry out to the living God, "Would you help us? Would you come and provide for us? Would you rebuke the destroyer and give us a game plan?" This is a work of God; He puts the love of God into our hearts, and He begins to save our children. The enemy will come in, and there will be a time in your life you will wonder if your home will survive. That is when you hold on, and just keep holding on, because the enemy does not want your children to survive. He does not want Christian homes to prosper because Christian men and women come from Christian homes, and they are the ones who know Jesus and can help transform a broken and fragmented society.

Will we stand in the gap for the next generation?

The little widow in Elisha's time stood in the gap, and her children were saved!

The Shunammite Woman

Now it happened one day that Elisha went to Shunem, where there was a notable woman, and she persuaded him to eat some food. So it was, as often as he passed by, he would turn in there to eat some food.

And she said to her husband, "Look now, I know that this is a holy man of God, who passes by us regularly. Please, let us make a small upper room on the wall; and let us put a bed for him there, and a table and a chair and a lampstand; so it will be, whenever he comes to us, he can turn in there."

And it happened one day that he came there, and he turned in to the upper room and lay down there. Then he said to Gehazi his servant, "Call this Shunammite woman." When he had called her, she stood before him. And he said to him, "Say now to her, 'Look, you have been concerned for us with all this care. What can I do for you? Do you want me to speak on your behalf to the king or to the commander of the army?'"

She answered, "I dwell among my own people."

So he said, "What then is to be done for her?" And Gehazi answered, "Actually, she has no son, and her husband is old."

So he said, "Call her." When he had called her, she stood in the doorway. Then he said, "About this time next year you shall embrace a son."

And she said, "No, my lord. Man of God, do not lie to your maidservant!"

But the woman conceived and bore a son when the appointed time had come, of which Elisha had told her (2 Kings 4:8-17).

We get halfway through the story of the Shunammite woman before we realize that she carried incredible pain in her heart. She had no child, and because of this she bore reproach in her society. This was not the first thing we learn about this woman. What we see first about her was her giving heart and her sensitivity to the needs of the prophet of the Lord. She let the living God take her pain, and she embraced Him in that pain. God gave her a special sensitivity to the needs of His prophet; she had a practical and compassionate heart for God's man. The tired prophet passed through her town as he journeyed from place to place, and she noticed that he needed somewhere to stop and rest. She asked him to come for a meal, and then he began to stop regularly for a meal every time he came through her town. Then, she had the good idea of making him a little room so that when he traveled through town, he had a place to rest on his journey. Doesn't it sound just like the home that Mary and Martha provided for Jesus? She set up a little "prophet's chamber," and she made sure that he had what he needed.

> *God is the God of every person, no matter the circumstances.*

The first woman in 2nd Kings 4 was incredibly poor, but this woman had money to spend, and she chose to spend it on the prophet. God is the God of every person, no matter the circumstances. He can meet the needs of both. The husband agreed to his wife's plan for the "prophet's chamber," and Scripture gives us all the details of what went lovingly into that little room.

The prophet, in his gratitude, looked at this woman who had provided for him, and said, "What can I do for you?" He volunteered to talk to the king on her behalf, which shows you how little he knows about the needs of her heart.

She responded by saying, "I have all that I need. What could the king do for me?" Elisha had no idea what gift would bless her, but his servant knew. He saw that this woman had no son, her husband was old, and so her hope for a family was gone. The servant told Elisha of the woman's need, and immediately Elisha called the woman and announced that God would give her a son.

Do you know how there are some moments that your memory just impresses on your mind and you never forget them? I remember exactly what I was wearing the day I first met Al; I was wearing a little blue sweater and a blue plaid skirt. It is just as clear in my mind as it can be. Something changed in my life on that day. I am sure this happened to the Shunammite woman at that moment. She stood in the doorway, and said to the prophet, "Don't lie to me." Her heart could not bear any more disappointment; how many times had she been disappointed in the past?

The Word of the Lord came to that generous woman in all His transforming power. It seemed too good to be true, but it was true. Jesus Christ comes to us today and says, "Behold, I can make all things new" (Revelation 21:5). The blood of Jesus cleanses us from all sin, and He can fill us with all the fullness of God. He can do abundantly more than we could ever ask or think. The Word of the Lord brings His blessing and His hope. The Shunammite woman could not believe it, but it was true, and God gave her a son. This woman had no ulterior motives in her care of the prophet. She simply opened her home and provided for God's prophet, and God gave her the hidden desire of her heart.

> *God is anxious to give us the desires of our hearts because He loves us and He made us to be full and complete in Him.*

Sometimes we forget that God made us, and He desires our fulfillment and our joy. He is anxious to give us the desires of our hearts because He loves us and He made us to be full and complete in Him. Our happiness is His concern. It is safe to trust Him with the desires that no one else knows; it is safe to wait on Him for His timing for those things.

The story of the Shunammite family continues in 2 Kings 4:18-25:

> *And the child grew. Now it happened one day that he went out to his father, to the reapers. And he said to his father, "My head, my head!" So he said to a servant, "Carry him to his mother."*
>
> *When he had taken him and brought him to his mother, he sat on her knees till noon, and then died. And she went up and laid him on the bed of the man of God, shut the door upon him, and went out. Then she called to her husband, and said, "Please send me one of the young men and one of the donkeys, that I may run to the man of God and come back."*
>
> *So he said, "Why are you going to him today? It is neither the New Moon nor the Sabbath."*
>
> *And she said, "It is well." Then she saddled a donkey, and said to her servant, "Drive, and go forward; do not slacken the pace for me unless I tell you." And so she departed, and went to the man of God at Mount Carmel.*
>
> *So it was, when the man of God saw her afar off, that he said to his servant Gehazi, "Look, the Shunammite woman!"*

That little son grew, and one day he was out in the fields with his daddy. His head began to hurt, and when he complained, his father sent him into the house with a servant. The seriousness of the little boy's condition was unknown to the parents until he died on his mama's lap at noon. In the morning, her son was alive and well, but by noon he was dead. The bereaved mama picked up that little boy and laid him on the bed in the prophet's chamber. She called for a donkey and set out for the prophet's house. When she arrived, Elisha did not know why she had come. She fell off the donkey at his feet, and she wrapped her arms around his sandals and said, "Did I ask a son of my Lord?" She refused to leave without Elisha.

Elisha went with her and came into his own room in this woman's house and closed the door. He began to pray over the boy, and he stretched out on the boy and walked around and prayed repeatedly. Finally, the little boy sneezed, and life came back into his body. Elisha called the woman. She knelt at the feet of the prophet, picked up her child, and left.

God wants to work His resurrection power in our lives and in our homes.

What I love about this story is the woman's determination. She declared to Elisha, "I did not ask for this child; he is God's gift to me. Therefore, God has an obligation to save his life!" She is desperate but not in despair. She knows where to go, and she holds on for the life of her son. It is interesting that she does not even inform her husband; she goes immediately to the man of God.

There are times when we must say, "Enough is enough." The enemy cannot have our homes, our families, or our children. Perhaps the situation looks like a dead situation; there may be no breath of life, but God wants to work His resurrection power in our lives and in our homes. This woman of faith determined not to make funeral preparations but to make resurrection plans. She was going to hold onto God and exhaust every avenue for God's Spirit to move in her situation. She was not going to let go until God Himself worked on her behalf. She reminds me of the Syrophoenician woman in the New Testament who was willing to be called a dog so long as Jesus healed her child.

Prayer Challenge

God is looking for people today who would be willing to hold on like that Shunammite woman. He wants us to claim our children and declare to Him, "We will not let you go until you bless us." God wants us to be willing to stand in the gap and hold on for the full blessing of God in the lives of our children, homes, and families in this generation and in the generations yet to come. This takes persistent and prevailing prayer and a belief that God can move and will act on our behalf. When we are in difficult situations and perhaps we want to get out, God says, "Hold on for my blessing! Hold on for my help." We are not planning funerals but resurrection celebrations!

He strengthens us when we are weary; He provides for us when we lack. He moves mountains and opens locked doors. He comforts us in trouble and gives wisdom and hope in difficult and dark places.

Many times, we do not want to pay the price of prayer. The Shunammite woman helps me here. She went to the prophet of God first; we do not have to go to the prophet, we can just go into God's immediate presence with our concerns for ourselves and our loved ones. As He becomes the hiding place for our hearts, we are free to love and give of ourselves. He strengthens us when we are weary; He provides for us when we lack. He moves mountains and opens locked doors. He comforts us in trouble and gives wisdom and hope in difficult and dark places. We are afraid to pay the price, but when we do, we find the wonder and joy of Jesus' immediate presence, help, comfort, and unending love. When we pull back from Him in fear, we find no place to turn with our burdens, pains, and struggles. When we die, we will not care if we had more money in our bank account, but we will care if our families are with us for eternity.

Are we willing to pay the price for the souls of our family and our friends? Only that is eternal!

It is costly, and it is hard, but as we begin to hold on to Jesus, we come to know Him.

Are we willing to pay that price so that redemption flows from our homes?

Maybe Jesus would like us to say, "I am willing to be your point person for these you have entrusted to me. I will run to you with my prayers, my questions, my burdens, and my cares."

George Verwer was a young high school kid from a non-Christian family. A woman in his town began to get a burden for high school students. She began to pray systematically and carefully for George. She prayed for a whole year. Then she prayed a second year. George became a Christian. She prayed another year, and George was filled with the Spirit. She prayed for four years, and revival broke out at George Verwer's high school. God began to put his hand on that kid and call him into ministry. George Verwer now heads Operation Mobilization, which has a worldwide impact for Christ. This woman touched the world for Jesus because she prayed consistently and faithfully for high school students.[6]

We do not have to travel the globe to make a difference for God. We can begin to invest in one or two other people and hold God's world in our hearts. We can pray for our communities, our families, our country, and our world. We can pray that God comes in revival!

> *We do not have to travel the globe to make a difference for God.*

I went to lunch with a friend, and she shared this verse with me:

By wisdom a house is built and through understanding it is established in knowledge. Its rooms are filled with rare and beautiful treasures (Proverbs 24:3-4).

As I went home, I pondered that verse.

What if God is calling us to do some spring cleaning in our souls and in our homes?

What if He is asking us to pray, "Jesus, I would like to make this home and my heart a reflection of who you are, and I just claim it for you. In each room of our house, both physical and spiritual, would you come with your rare and beautiful treasures of wisdom, knowledge and understanding"?

This is what Titus 2 is all about. Titus 2:1-5 has gripped me ever since I have begun working with women in ministry. It is so practical and engages the whole woman. It details how we allow our lives and our homes to be filled with the wisdom and knowledge that come from the Holy Spirit.

1. Older women, teach the younger women to love their husbands. Are we lovers of our husbands? Do we love them creatively and in the Spirit of Jesus?

2. Love your children. Do we really love our children? Or do we just love them because they are ours? Children are incredibly important to the heart of God. Does Jesus love our children through us?

3. Be sensible. Are we sensible? How can Jesus make us practical and faithful in the details of life?

4. Be pure. Are we pure? We cannot expect purity in others unless we are pure. What do we watch on TV? I cannot overemphasize that what you put into your mind is what will come out. What we sow, our children will reap. If we sow little sins, our children will reap a whirlwind of sin. The beautiful thing is

that Jesus can make us pure. He can cleanse us from all sin so we are creative and loving homemakers.

5. Be kind. The second verse I had my children memorize was Ephesians 4:32, "Be kind to one another, tenderhearted, forgiving one another, even as God in Christ has forgiven you." Are we forgiving? Do we harbor bitterness?

6. Be submissive. I did not add this to Scripture, God did. There needs to come into our lives a willingness to lay down our rights. He wants us to be honest and open, but He does not want us to insist on our own way. The happiest thing in the world is the freedom of not having to have your own way. We can let Jesus meet our needs and live for His approval and His alone.

Jesus wants to fill our lives with rare and beautiful treasures. He cannot do it unless we are all His and unless we allow His resurrection life to flow through us.

Is there anything in your life or home that needs to be thrown out?

We must be crucified with Christ, so that His life can flow through us, and we can know the fellowship of His sufferings. If we are going to know Jesus Christ, we must die—not to our personhood—but to our self-will, self-absorption, and selfishness. We must let Jesus Christ come and meet the deepest needs of our lives. Then, when adversities come with trials, pain, and suffering, we can embrace Him in the midst of those and out of our lives can flow the sweetness of Jesus. We become like the Shunammite woman who could see the needs of others because she was not focusing on her own needs. We can become more patient, more gentle, and more compassionate because of the presence of Jesus Himself in our suffering.

If we are going to know Jesus Christ, we must die—not to our personhood—but to our self-will, self-absorption, and selfishness.

My prayer has become, "Jesus, I would like to invite you into my kitchen. I give you my teacups and plates. Could you use them for your kingdom? Could you touch my culinary skills for your glory? Jesus, I invite you into my neighborhood. Could you touch my neighbors with your Good News? Could you use me? Jesus, would you decorate my house and make me creative? Let my home be a place where Jesus is welcome and present." Jesus is so creative and practical; He wants to help us with all the practical aspects of daily life.

Is Jesus Lord of your life? Lord of your home?

Are we borrowing oil pots for the overflow? Or are we giving our sons away?

Are we planning resurrections or are we planning funerals?

Jesus offers abundant life if we simply come to Him and receive it.

Personal Reflection

What are the needs of your heart today? Is the creditor after your children? Do you have a burden on your heart to pray for your family, to intercede for them until God breaks through in their lives? If so, write the names of your family members here and ask Jesus to begin to give you specific verses and promises to claim for each child, friend, relative, spouse.

When we face disappointments and deeply personal pain, where do we run? Are you running to Jesus for His answer, His provision, His hope? Take some time to look at those places of pain and disappointment in your life. Invite Jesus into those places and ask Him to bring healing and hope to your own heart and family.

Notes

Notes

CHAPTER
6

A TRANSFORMED HEART / A COVETOUS HEART

CHAPTER 6 — A TRANSFORMED HEART/ A COVETOUS HEART

*O*ur story has been taking place in Israel, and now we turn to the country of Syria and to the commander of the army of Syria, a man named Naaman. He was great and honorable, and his master was very proud of him because the Lord had given victory to Syria. The Scripture says that it was the Lord who gave Syria the victories. Who is the great controller of all things? God himself. Who is the one who controls on the international stage? God himself. There are no second causes. God had given Syria the victory. Every place Naaman had gone, Syria won its battles. Naaman was an astute soldier and an honorable man. He was a mighty man of valor. He was gifted and equipped, helping Syria to become an international power.

Who is the great controller of all things? God Himself.

As Syria grew in power, Israel's power on the international scene began to disappear. Jerusalem was a little less cultured, a little less powerful, and a little less impressive than Damascus in all its beauty. Damascus, the capital of Syria, was built upon an oasis, famous for its beauty. Naturally, Naaman had pride in his own country and a little disdain for Israel. And then something occurred in Naaman's life that nothing could help—not power, not sophistication, not the King of Syria himself. Naaman contracted leprosy. In those days leprosy was a death sentence, and anyone who had leprosy was the outcast of society, separated from home, work, and family. This man of all worldly power had nothing to meet this need.

The Witness of a Child

> *Now Naaman, commander of the army of the king of Syria, was a great and honorable man in the eyes of his master, because by him the LORD had given victory to Syria. He was also a mighty man of valor, but a leper. And the Syrians had gone out on raids, and had brought back captive a young girl from the land of Israel. She waited on Naaman's wife. Then she said to her mistress, "If only my master were with the prophet who is in Samaria! For he would heal him of his leprosy (2 Kings 5:1-3).*

So often in the goodness of God, He allows the trials of life to be difficult enough that we begin to realize there are needs of heart, body, and soul that we cannot meet. When God permitted life's circumstances to awaken Naaman to his own need, he also provided an answer (as He often does) in the words and love of a child. In fact, God brought in a little Israelite child to be the bearer of God's good news.

In Naaman's home, a little slave girl served his wife. She was a conquest from a Syrian raid against Israel. Somehow, this unnamed girl knew the painful secret that Naaman was a leper. One day she worked up her courage to share with her mistress a secret hope. I think it is an indication of Naaman's generosity of spirit that this little girl wanted to help her master, even though he was responsible for removing her from her home. She rallied her courage and went to her mistress and told her that there lived a prophet in Israel who could cleanse Naaman of the dreaded disease. I am sure with excitement, Naaman's wife told her husband what the servant girl had said, and Naaman agreed to go to the prophet of Samaria.

As we read the story, we understand that this man moved among kings and the highest levels of society. He was a powerful man in the kingdom of Syria. The God of Israel invited Naaman to tread through the valley of humiliation, perhaps testing Naaman to see if his pride or his need would win the day. First, he had to take wisdom from a child—an Israelite child, no less. Naaman humbly submitted to the wisdom of a child, and she pointed him to the only hope she knew—to the prophet of God in Israel.

There is a story that I love to read, and I read it to my children when they were little. It is a precious children story about a little boy named Tom who lived in East London.[7] He was a crippled orphan boy whose parents had died when he was a baby. He stayed with a woman whom he called granny, but he was not actually related to her. She took care of his physical needs, but she was cross and grumpy. He seemed to be just waiting to die. As he lay in his little bed, he became very hungry to know God like his mother had known God. One day, a friend named Nick came up the back steps to his room carrying a brown paper bag with some money in it.

"I am going away. I think I can make more money on the north side of London, so I am headed out. I did not want to leave without telling you good-bye and giving you some money that I have saved. I would like to buy you a present before I go."

Tom looked at him, and he said, "I know exactly what I want, and I know exactly where it is. Would you run down the street and at the little corner store, there is a Bible; would you go buy me that Bible?"

Nick said, "Really? I worked all this time to give you a Bible? I don't know anything about the Bible. Why do you want a Bible? I thought you might want something exciting."

"No, please," said Tom. "I don't know if you understand it or not, but I think in the Bible there might be something that could give me hope as I lie here in this bed." Nick reluctantly took his coppers and ran down the street. There was a little Bible at the corner shop. He ran back up the stairs happily because he was able to give a gift to his friend Tom. He gave the Bible to Tom, and Tom never saw him again. Tom hugged that Bible to his heart, and then he began to read that Bible day after day after day, learning the story of Jesus' love for him.

The minute one really begins to get a transformed heart one begins to get out of one's comfort zone and think of others.

It was not long before he found Jesus Christ in the pages of John, and he opened up his heart to the Lord Jesus. His life was transformed. The minute one really begins to get a transformed heart one begins to get out of one's comfort zone and think of others. Tom said to himself, "I need to reach out to someone else now. How can I do that?" He could not walk, and he could not leave his room. He asked Granny if he could have a pencil and some papers, and she reluctantly gave them to him. He began to take Scripture verses and write them out. Then, he would drop them out his window, and they fell on the street below him. Day after day Tom wrote Scripture verses and dropped out portions of Scripture on the street below.

Tom did not know what happened to those portions of Scripture. Nobody responded. Faithfully little Tom would write the Scripture verses and drop them out the window, praying over them. One day he heard a strange step coming up the back steps to his room. There was a knock at the door, and a man came in. Tom did not know the man, but he was carrying one of the portions of Scripture, and he said, "Little boy, did you give me this?"

"Yes, I did." Tom replied. "God's word has so changed my life. I just have to share it and I thought maybe if just one person could read it and know God's love for them, I would be happy." The stranger said, "I was walking along and felt something fall on the top of the brim of my hat. I reached up, and it was your Scripture verse, "Repent and be converted that your sins may be blotted out." He said, "I knew Jesus when I was young, but I've lost my love for him. I've gotten into the good life. I'm a wealthy man. I've got an estate in the country. I'm a big-time businessman, but I have forgotten the One who loved me and died for me."

> *God is calling us to Himself, to allow ourselves to be transformed by His Word, to allow that Word to take root in our own lives and slosh into the lives of others.*

"Mister, it's not too late. Let's just pray right now." Little Tom led that man to Jesus right in his upper room. The man was so touched that he asked Tom to come and live with him, but little Tom said, "I have to stay here and share God's Word with East London until Jesus comes and takes me home."

Like the Good Samaritan, the manmade provision with the grumpy granny to take care of Tom in a fashion that he had never known, and it was not too much longer when he received in the mail Tom's Bible and a note from Granny saying that Tom had passed into the presence of Jesus.

That little Bible was so full of Tom's notes and his love letters and prayers to Jesus that the man took it and shared it with his son. The son found Christ, and he said, "I have to go and share the Good News of God in Africa through Bible translation." A little boy transformed by the Word of God, a father transformed by the Word of God, a son transformed by the Word of God, and the Word of God translated into an unknown language. Eternity was changed because of little Tom and his Bible.

> *Eternity was changed because of one little boy and his Bible.*

One child witnessed of the living God to Naaman's wife, and an important Syrian general who had access to the King of Syria found healing and salvation. God is calling us to Himself, to allow ourselves to be transformed by His Word, to allow that Word to take root in our own lives and slosh into the lives of others. I think God is calling us as women to begin to train younger women in new ways, so we begin to strengthen others to know Jesus and love Him with all their hearts.

The Valley of Humiliation

The story continues in 2 Kings 5:4-8.

> *Naaman went to his master and told him what the girl from Israel had said. "By all means, go," the king of Aram replied. "I will send a letter to the king of Israel." So Naaman left, taking with him ten talents of silver, six thousand shekels of gold and ten sets of clothing. The letter that he took to the king of Israel read: "With this letter I am sending my servant Naaman to you so that you may cure him of his leprosy."*
>
> *As soon as the king of Israel read the letter, he tore his robes and said, "Am I God? Can I kill and bring back to life? Why does this fellow send someone to me to be cured of his leprosy? See how he is trying to pick a quarrel with me!" When Elisha the man of God heard that the king of Israel had torn his robes, he sent him this message: "Why have you torn your robes? Have the man come to me and he will know that there is a prophet in Israel."*

Naaman still had to walk through another valley of humiliation. He had to humble himself, not only before a child, but also when he arrived in Israel. At first, he said, "I will go to the King of Israel. That is where I will be healed." He was accustomed to places of power, and he confidently assumed the God of Israel would heal him in the court of the king. He brought his impressive entourage, his wealthy gifts, and he went to the source of power in Israel—or rather, the seeming source of power. However, the king of Israel was as powerless as Naaman himself and immediately became angry with the presumption that he had the power to heal leprosy. In his anger, he assumed the Syrian king was setting a trap. Before disaster occurred in the court of the king, Elisha heard that Naaman had come and sent word to the king that Naaman should be sent to him. Gratefully, the king of Israel sent Naaman to the house of Elisha the prophet.

Undaunted, Naaman willingly went to see Elisha with all his pomp and circumstance. He arrived outside the small house with many changes of clothes, ten thousand shekels of gold, and a retinue of servants. He brought it all to Elisha's house as gifts for the healing arts Elisha would perform. Elisha did not even bother to come to the door. He never saw Naaman's wealth or gifts or servants. He simply told his servant to instruct the Syrian general to wash in the River Jordan seven times and be cleansed.

> So Naaman went with his horses and chariots and stopped at the door of Elisha's house. Elisha sent a messenger to say to him, "Go, wash yourself seven times in the Jordan, and your flesh will be restored, and you will be cleansed."
>
> But Naaman went away angry and said, "I thought that he would surely come out to me and stand and call on the name of the Lord his God, wave his hand over the spot and cure me of my leprosy. Are not Abana and Pharpar, the rivers of Damascus, better than all the waters of Israel? Couldn't I wash in them and be cleansed?" So, he turned and went off in a rage.
>
> Naaman's servants went to him and said, "My father, if the prophet had told you to do some great thing, would you not have done it? How

much more, then, when he tells you, 'Wash and be cleansed'!" So, he went down and dipped himself in the Jordan seven times, as the man of God had told him, and his flesh was restored and became clean like that of a young boy.

Naaman had about all the humiliation he could bear. He was furious. He did not want to wash in the Jordan River. He did not want to be ignored by the prophet. He did not want to take direction from a servant. He was angry, and I am sure embarrassed. It was humiliating to admit he had leprosy to the king and then to the prophet and then to the prophet's servant. Naaman could not bear the pain of the humiliation, and he pulled out in anger to return to Syria.

> *Only the blood of Jesus cleanses us from all sin and heals, and it is available to every single person.*

Our God is not a bit impressed when we come to Him on our terms. When we say, "Lord, I will come and meet you, but I want to come on my terms." God says, "No, if you come to me and if you're going to wash and be cleansed, there is only one way to wash and be cleansed, and it is through the shed blood of Jesus Christ. There is no other way. I am not impressed by power. I am not impressed by prestige. I am not impressed by money. My cleansing is for everyone— whosoever will come." Only the blood of Jesus cleanses us from all sin and heals from all wounds, and it is available to every single person. Somehow, He allows the difficulties in our lives that will force us to decide between His way and our own.

Like many of us, Naaman almost missed the cleansing power of God in his life because of p-r-i-d-e.

We do not want to submit our pride to Christ. We do not want to surrender to Him because we do not want to be ashamed, or embarrassed or different from others. We want to have options. We do not want to let people know we have a need, and we do not want to let God know. We would like to get into the kingdom, but we would like to get into the kingdom without suffering any humiliation or loss of face or sense of need. God comes as the great equalizer and declares that the cross is available for every man, woman, and child. The blood of Jesus can cleanse us from all sin. All leprosy can be put under the blood, and we can walk out a new person in Christ, but there needs to be a humbling of our pride before the Eternal God.

I love the response of Naaman's servants. They came to him respectfully, and I get the sense that they really loved their master. They did not want him to return home with leprosy, and so hesitantly but boldly they confronted him, "My father, if the prophet had told you to do some great thing, would you not have done it? How much more, then, when he tells you, 'Wash and be cleansed'!" The servants gently reminded Naaman of the commonsense nature of the request. He would have done something great and difficult, but all that was asked of him was to wash and be clean.

There are moments when God speaks His instructions into our lives, not difficult, but still we turn away when He calls our name. Obedience seems to come at a cost. He is asking us,

"Do you want to be made well?"

We always seem to be sitting in the back row when God calls our name. My husband, Al, was sitting on the back row in a camp meeting with his girlfriend and his best friend when God called him and said, "This is your hour. This is the time."

He said, "Oh no, God. Not from the back row during an evening service. Can't you wait until nobody is here...Just you and me?" God did not wait, and neither did Al. He moved past the girlfriend and past the friends and walked down to that altar and gave all his life to God. A moment will come for all of us when God will say,

"This is the time. Are you willing to humble yourself and come to me?

Are you willing to let me take care of your pride?

Are you willing to accept my sacrifice for you?"

A Humble Heart

Naaman submitted. Down into the water seven times, the number of completion. When he came up out of the water for the seventh time, his skin was as clean as a baby's skin. He was healed of his leprosy. Overwhelmed with emotion and gratitude, Naaman rushed back to the prophet Elisha, and Elisha came out to meet him. The surrender had been made; the healing had come, and the prophet of God rejoiced in it wholeheartedly. Naaman was overflowing with thankfulness. That is what happens to the human heart, healed from sin and brokenness—just like little Tom, we become desperate to show our gratitude. Naaman expressed his thanksgiving in the only way that he knew how: he offered lavish gifts to express his gratitude to the God of Elisha.

And he returned to the man of God, he and all his aides, and came and stood before him; and he said, "Indeed, now I know that there is no God in all the earth, except in Israel; now therefore, please take a gift from your servant." But he said, "As the LORD lives, before whom I stand, I will receive nothing." And he urged him to take it, but he refused.

So Naaman said, "Then, if not, please let your servant be given two mule-loads of earth; for your servant will no longer offer either burnt offering or sacrifice to other gods, but to the LORD. Yet in this thing may the LORD pardon your servant: when my master goes into the temple of Rimmon to worship there, and he leans on my hand, and I bow down in the temple of Rimmon—when I bow down in the temple of Rimmon, may the LORD please pardon your servant in this thing."

Then he said to him, "Go in peace." So he departed from him a short distance.

> We cannot buy or sell the grace of God. It is a free gift available to us.

Elisha had a squeaky clean heart, and he had no desire for Naaman's wealth or gifts. This was not about Elisha's power but about the God of Israel, and he did not want to take anything that would confuse that reality. He refused the offered presents and said, "No, I will take nothing. This is a gift from the God of Israel." We cannot buy or sell the grace of God. It is a free gift available to us.

I love the next part of this story: Naaman humbled himself further and asked the poor prophet for a gift. He requested two loads of dirt from Israel so that he could build an altar to the Living God and worship that God in his home country of Syria. Then he asked permission to escort the king of Syria into the temple of his god. One of his responsibilities was to walk with the king into the temple of the Syrian gods, and Naaman was anxious that the God of Israel would be offended by this act of service to the king. Elisha gave the dirt for the altar and the permission to escort the king, and he sent him off with peace, healing and joy. Elisha saw the loyal heart of Naaman, and he responded to him with grace and love.

Naaman returned to Syria, a worshipper of the living God with dirt from Israel to make an altar. His heart had become the heart of one who followed Elisha's God. God will go to any lengths to get His witness in the highest places in the land. I am sure the King of Syria looked at him and said, "You are well! Thank the gods!"

I can imagine Naaman saying, "Actually, I will thank the God of Israel. Only He has the power to heal and to save."

Can't you hear the king of Syria saying to his most respected military leader, "Really? Tell me what you learned about Him." God got a witness to the King of Syria.

Where is your heart today?

Is your heart one that follows no matter the cost?

Have you surrendered your pride?

The little Israeli handmaiden who witnessed to the God of Israel without bitterness or anger desired to see her Syrian master healed. The love of her God flowed out in love even for those who held her captive. God's love is like that; it is almost as if we cannot keep it down or hold it back. It sloshes out in the most painful and difficult circumstances because it is His love. As Naaman walked through the valley of humiliation, he encountered the God of Israel who brought healing and wholeness to his body and life, and in the process God's witness was given to the nation of Syria.

> *God's love sloshes out in the most painful and difficult circumstances because it is His love.*

A Covetous Heart

> *But Gehazi, the servant of Elisha the man of God, said, "Look, my master has spared Naaman this Syrian, while not receiving from his hands what he brought; but as the LORD lives, I will run after him and take something from him." So Gehazi pursued Naaman. When Naaman saw him running after him, he got down from the chariot to meet him, and said, "Is all well?"*
>
> *And he said, "All is well. My master has sent me, saying, 'Indeed, just now two young men of the sons of the prophets have come to me from the mountains of Ephraim. Please give them a talent of silver and two changes of garments.'"*

So Naaman said, "Please, take two talents." And he urged him, and bound two talents of silver in two bags, with two changes of garments, and handed them to two of his servants; and they carried them on ahead of him (2 Kings 5:20-23).

The prophet's servant, Gehazi, was in full-time Christian service with the leading prophet in all of Israel at that time. He served Elisha and had a front row seat to all that God was doing through Elisha. He watched Naaman's miraculous healing. He saw the scene unfold as Naaman came back to say thank you, and he observed the incredible wealth of Naaman. He listened with surprise as Elisha refused the gifts of Syria, and he watched the coins of gold and the beautiful clothing begin the long journey back to Syria. As he looked on these events, a covetous spirit rose in his heart. An ugly spirit of need and grasping desire was born in his heart. (I think Gehazi already had sin in his heart, particularly because the little Shunammite woman in the last chapter would not trust Gehazi to pray over her son. He had no power in his spiritual life.) Gehazi was in Christian service. He seemed to be a loyal servant of the living God of Elisha, but he had a treacherous heart underneath. He concocted a scheme for a way to get the gifts of Naaman for himself.

Instead of rejoicing with Elisha about the healing of Naaman, Gehazi decided to grab a golden opportunity for himself. His covetous heart resulted in a deceitful and lying tongue. As soon as the Syrian general began his trip home, Gehazi snuck out the door of the prophet's cottage in pursuit. Eventually, Gehazi flagged down Naaman, and out of breath, he gasped out a lie. "The prophet has had some friends come to stay with him, and he is asking for a bit of money and a change of clothes for his friends."

Naaman, not knowing the heart of the servant, gave gladly and contributed even more than was asked. Gehazi greedily received Naaman's proffered help and then skulked home to hide Naaman's gifts, pretending that nothing had happened. Like many Christians today, Gehazi believed that he could have the favor of the prophet's God and the wealth of the Syrian. Of course, he did not want to give up God altogether. He thought he could live with a divided heart, getting what he wanted while living for God. This, however, does not work and always shows the ugliness, the smallness, and the conniving nature of one's heart. Often, that is the case with us. We believe we can live with a little lie or a little greed or a little manipulation. Little do we know what the effects of this sin will be.

> *When we walk with God, He gives us a spirit of discernment and wisdom.*

Elisha was not fooled by Gehazi's lie; he had seen the greedy look in his servant's eye. When we walk with God, He gives us a spirit of discernment and wisdom. He makes His people "wise as serpents and innocent as doves." When Gehazi returned from stowing away the goods, Elisha looked at him and said, "Did not my heart go with you when the man turned back from his chariot to meet you? Is it time to receive money and to receive clothing, olive groves and vineyards, sheep and oxen, male and female servants? Therefore, the leprosy of Naaman shall cling to you and your descendants forever." And it was so.

Before Gehazi could leave the room, the leprosy of Naaman was upon him, and he became an exile. God will not tolerate a divided heart; if we have a covetous spirit, it will be revealed. God, in His love, will allow us the consequences of our greed, and He will expose it.

How often we can be in full-time Christian service and lose our first love. The book of Revelation is full of warnings about this. When we begin to listen to the lies of the enemy and become dissatisfied with God's will, we quickly spiral into a selfishness that causes pain to those we love. We must keep our hearts on fire for Jesus with a passion for Him; we must keep short accounts with Him and with others.

A friend called me recently and said, "I believe Jesus is showing me how the enemy can get a stronghold in our lives and in the lives of those we love when we begin to *play with the truth* instead of *living in God's truth*." When we begin to entertain a covetous heart in our self-talk, that is all hell needs to move into our souls and minds. That is exactly what happened in the Garden of Eden. The serpent planted

> *God does not want cookie cutter followers. God loves every single person.*

just a little doubt about the goodness of God in the mind of Eve, and disaster resulted!

Perhaps we get into full time Christian service and realize that we have more month than money, and our hearts are tempted to grow covetous. We begin to whine a little, "This is hard Jesus, if we could just pay the bills and have a little extra." So, we begin to doubt the goodness of God instead of letting God transform our situations.

Another favorite lie of the enemy concerns our own self-image. We often think, "I just wish I was thinner or curvier or prettier or brighter or smarter or taller or shorter." We get unhappy with who we are and where we are. Guard your heart! Guard your mind! Ask Jesus to give you His perspective on your body, your personality, your gifts, and your weaknesses. God does not want to have cookie cutter followers. God loves every single person. Our prayer should be, "Jesus, let me be the woman you have made me to be!" He does not want every single woman to be a size 4 or 6. God says, "I want you to be who I made you to be." Don't let your standard for beauty be the world's standard, let it be God's standard.

> *There is a freedom and a joy in being exactly who Jesus made you to be at exactly this time in your life.*

If we do not guard our hearts, we will move into the realm of self-pity; dissatisfaction with ourselves will cause continual anxiety and strain. There is a freedom and a joy in being exactly who Jesus made you to be at exactly this time in your life. Our prayer can be, "Jesus, you have given me my gifts and talents because you have a purpose for my life; I chose to rejoice in your plan for me!" Jesus has made us exactly how we are mentally, physically, emotionally, spiritually, and psychologically. I love Romans 12:1-3:

> *"Present your bodies a living sacrifice, holy and acceptable to God. Do not be conformed to this world but be transformed by the renewing of your minds...think soberly about yourself."*

Then Romans 12 goes on to talk about all the different gifts of God. We have the freedom through the Holy Spirit to resist the lies of the enemy that declare what a failure we are and throw us into the depths of self-pity and depression. We are free to say, "I am not going to hear your lies to me one more day. Not one more day."

2 Corinthians 10 gives the strategy for defeating the enemy's lies:

> *"For the weapons of our warfare are not carnal but mighty in God for pulling down strongholds, casting down arguments and every high thing that exalts itself against the knowledge of God, bringing every thought into captivity and obedience to Jesus Christ"* (10:4-5).

Let's begin to say to Jesus, "I want to be yours, every cell and every chromosome.

Will you help me to be exactly who you want me to be?

I want to be free to stop thinking of myself and begin to think about other people." Remember what Tom did after Jesus touched his heart: he began to share God's word with other people. God has made you, and He loves you. He wants you to love Him in return. Only you can love Him as you, so He is waiting for you. If you were not here, there would be a hole in the heart of God. No one can love Jesus Christ like you can love Him. He has not

God has made you and He loves you. He wants you to love Him in return.

made anyone the same because He wants us to find in Him our perfection and fulfillment. He wants us to look to Him and not to the world. He wants to keep us free so that we do not live in bondage to the enemy's lies!

I remember the day I realized I was more devoted to my personal happiness than I was to God or to my husband. How well the enemy had masked my self-centeredness behind false holiness. When I prayed that positive changes would fill my husband's life, it was because I wanted those benefits for myself, not for his sake, much less for the glory of Jesus Christ. I prayed for him because I wanted to be more comfortable. I found myself surprised and offended by God when He did not work in the way I wanted Him to work. I found myself praying, "God, this is not what I expected. This isn't how I thought You would work in my life. You are not being fair to me!" When there is pain in our lives and circumstances do not change for the better, we find the temptation to grow sullen or afraid and walk away from Him. What He wants us to do is walk to Him, to embrace Him in that pain and let Him transform us and make us more like Himself. Then He can make us useful for the kingdom and for others.

God wants us to walk to Him, to embrace Him in our pain and let Him transform us and make us more like Himself.

Jesus Christ can meet every single need of our hearts, and He can work circumstances for His honor and glory, but we must get honest and say, "Jesus, I am going to look to you to meet the needs of my heart. I'm going to look to you to transform my life. I'm going to look to you to make me a woman after God's own heart; I am going to stop looking around, and I am going to stop believing the lies of the enemy."

God wants us to be holy as He is holy. He will take care of us so that we can live in love with others.

The enemy will come and say, "You deserve better than this! You need to get out of this marriage, or you need to walk away from this child that has hurt you. God wants you to be happy; you have to take care of yourself." This is a lie. God wants us to be holy as He is holy. He will take care of us so that we can live in love with others. That very person that you cannot stand, whether it is a husband or a roommate, a co-worker or a missionary, that very one is a gift from God. As God transforms you to be able to have Calvary love and Trinity unity, that relationship that has been full of thorns can become the sweetest bunch of red roses by His grace and His love.

Is it painful? Yes!

Costly? Yes!

Eternal? Yes and yes!

Fruitful. Yes!

Life-changing? Yes!

Fulfilling? Yes!

We begin to experience the incredible joy of the full will of God in our lives, no matter our circumstances.

The only other option is to try and live for Jesus with a covetous heart like Gehazi. We can live in a religious environment; we can talk all about Jesus, but our hearts can be as leprous as Gehazi's. God punished Gehazi by letting what was in his heart be revealed on the outside of his heart. All judgment will be this way; what is inside of us will be revealed for all the world to see. The very thing that we kept hidden away will eat our life from the inside out. We can look very religious for a while but be as worldly and covetous on the inside as it is possible to be, and sometime soon, there will be a Day of Reckoning for all of us! We must come to the place where our heart is all God's. We cannot fool Him.

> *We must come to the place where our heart is all God's heart.*

Where is your heart today?

Have you ever eaten a Cadbury Easter Egg? The delicious treat with the gooey middle? Cadbury was an Englishman; he had eight children and was an ardent Christian. He founded the Cadbury chocolate business. Many people in England at that time were struggling with alcohol addictions, and so he asked God to give him an idea to give people something else to drink. God gave him the idea of chocolate milk, and it proved an instant success. Cadbury worked in the city mission, and he was involved in children's ministry. One night, he took his sixth child, a little girl, to the city mission with him. In that place, among the drunks and drug addicts, she found Jesus and invited Him into her life. She also became an ardent little soul winner, and she took her Bible with her to school. She put it in her desk a little sheepishly and then waited for her moment to share Jesus. At lunchtime, her best friend, Claire, came up to her and said, "Why do you have that great big book in your desk?"

And she said "Well, it's a Bible."

"Oh," said Claire sarcastically, "I don't want any sermons. I have already been to church."

"I don't want to tell you a sermon. Let me just read you some verses." Little Miss Cadbury began to read from Romans 3,

> For all have sinned and come short of the glory of God.... for the wages of sin is death.

Claire went home thinking about those verses and the next day, she was back saying, "I would like to know Jesus as well." The two girls became a prayer team for that school. They asked God for a way to be able to bring the Bible to school because they felt there was such power in the Word, but they didn't know how to do it. The Bible seemed so big and heavy to carry around. Then Mr. Cadbury came up with the idea of pocket Testaments, small versions of the New Testament that would fit in anyone's pocket. Claire and Elizabeth began to sew pockets on their dresses for the New Testaments. They formed the Pocket Testament League. At the end of their time in school sixty children had found the Lord and joined the Pocket Testament League.

When she went to the university, she met a beautiful teacher named Mrs. Robertson. She became her English teacher, and she asked Elizabeth, "What books do you read?"

"Oh," she said with pleasure, "the one I love most is the Bible."

Her beautiful teacher smiled at her in a patronizing way and said, "I believe parts of the Bible too, but many aspects of it are outdated and irrelevant." This was a new thought for Elizabeth Cadbury. In her mind, she began to question her love for the Scripture, "Oh my, well, maybe I'm a fool, maybe just my dad believes like this." She began to read less and less of the Word of God and she began to witness less and less. It began as a little lie, but that lie began to snowball into doubts and confusion, and by the end of her college career, she had lost her faith. Her parents were grieved over this, and so her daddy proposed an Egyptian and Israeli tour for her graduation present. They packed up and headed to the Holy Land. The very first night that they were overseas, her daddy had a heart attack and died. Elizabeth and her mother came home brokenhearted. Elizabeth looked at all the books her English teacher had recommended; she looked at her geography books, history books, philosophy books, but there was only one book that her soul longed for, and it was God's Word. She began to open up the Scriptures again, and God brought her back to Himself.

It was not too long before she met a young song evangelist who had come to England. She fell in love with him, and they were married and began to do evangelism together. One day her husband said to her, "I wish we had a way to get Scriptures into the hands of people, so that it could transform their lives, but we need something small." Elizabeth thought back to her father and the little New Testaments for pockets, and she said to her husband, "I know a way to do it." They revitalized the Pocket Testament League.[8]

That organization has now been giving away pocket Testaments to people that they might know Jesus Christ for over a hundred years. It started in a heart of a little girl who found God and wanted to share Him.

As we bring ourselves to Him in openness, faith, and obedience, then He can make our lives a blessing to the world!

God wants to transform our hearts! He desires to take out the covetous and conniving nature that was in Gehazi and give us the humility and obedience of Naaman. Only God can do this, but He can as we bring ourselves to Him in openness, faith, and obedience, and then He can make our lives a blessing to the world!

Personal Reflection

Are you giving witness to the power of Christ to set people free and bring His salvation into their lives like the little girl in this story? Ask Jesus where are the places you could give your witness?

Are you willing to obey, even if your pride is hurt? Where are the places that you shrink from obedience because of your own stubbornness?

Is Christian activity in your life a cover for a greedy heart? Take some time to let the Holy Spirit uncover any covetousness in you and cleanse your heart. He can do it if you will give Him permission.

Notes

Notes

Notes

CHAPTER
7

THE THREE
MINI-MIRACLES

*O*ne of my favorite lessons of scripture comes from the Three Mighty Mini-Miracles that God does through Elisha's life. I ran across a book that my husband had on his shelf by Ronald Wallace. Ronald Wallace taught at Edinburgh, and the title of the book is *Elijah and Elisha*.[9] This little volume has been a gold mine for my heart. The outline for this chapter is not original with me. It comes from Ronald Wallace.

Wallace said that there are three miracles that God has slipped into Holy Scripture to encourage men and women in the Christian faith, and especially those who are trying to live for Jesus Christ with all their hearts and those in full-time Christian service. We can take heart because we serve a Christ who is in control of our mistakes, in control of our inadequacies, in control of the accidents that occur in our lives and ultimately in control of the universe. The expectation for those in Christian ministry is often perfection of performance or spectacular results, and the burden on believers can become unbearable. The Christian has the beautiful privilege of knowing the One who can take mistakes, inadequacies, and accidents and redeem them. He is the One who makes all things new and who uses

> *We have the beautiful privilege of knowing the One who can take mistakes, inadequacies, and accidents and redeem them.*

anything offered in love for Him for His own eternal purposes.

God's people can live knowing that there is victory as we serve God, not with perfection of performance, but with a blameless and pure heart. John Wesley declared that Christians can have a pure heart, one that belongs completely to God. It does not mean that we practice our faith perfectly, but that our heart is all His, and to the best of our knowledge there is no sin in our life. We refuse to live with hidden closets or places where there is any residue of sin.

Just like the Lord said to Samuel, "The Lord does not see as man sees; for man looks on the outward appearance, but the Lord looks on the heart" (1 Samuel 16:7). He says to believers that He is pleased with any love gift offered to Him, no matter the results.

> *God is pleased with any love gift offered to Him, no matter the results.*

I remember when one of my children was especially little, and she was learning to put on her own shoes. She loved wearing her Mary Jane shoes with pretty dresses, so when she got old enough she began to work on being able to put her black Sunday shoes on by herself. One morning, I found her sitting in the family room; she was working and working to get those little black shiny shoes on her feet. When she finished, she came to me and stood there in all her glory and said, "Mommy, look, I got my shoes on!" I looked down at her tiny feet and sure enough her shoes were on, but even after all that hard work, they were on the wrong feet. What do you think I said to her as her mama? Did I scold her? Correct her? Ridicule her?

Oh no! I said, "I am so proud of you! You did a beautiful job, and you just look lovely in your Mary Janes!" Happily, she ran off to play, and as she ran off Jesus spoke to my heart, "Bethie, you don't need to serve me with perfection of performance because you cannot. Just like your little one, you are trying your best to love me and sometimes you end up with your shoes on the wrong feet. Don't worry! I am not looking at the performance. I am looking at your heart. All I need is a surrendered heart." He is God over our mistakes. God is more loving to His children than the most loving mother or father. Isn't that good news? These three little miracles give a winsome picture of the heart of God towards His people and His tender care for them.

We don't have to serve with perfection of performance because we can't.

Miracle Number 1: Lord of our Mistakes

And Elisha returned to Gilgal, and there was a famine in the land. Now the sons of the prophets were sitting before him; and he said to his servant, "Put on the large pot, and boil stew for the sons of the prophets." So one went out into the field to gather herbs, and found a wild vine, and gathered from it a lapful of wild gourds, and came and sliced them into the pot of stew, though they did not know what they were. Then they served it to the men to eat.

Now it happened, as they were eating the stew, that they cried out and said, "Man of God, there

*is death in the pot!" And they could not eat it.
So he said, "Then bring some flour." And he put
it into the pot, and said, "Serve it to the people,
that they may eat." And there was nothing
harmful in the pot (4:38-41).*

Elisha had just returned from the Shunammite's
home where he raised her son from the dead; he came
back to meet with his Seminary students. Elijah was
a solitary prophet, but the prophet Elisha was busy
making disciples. He had raised up a whole group of
young prophets, and he was in the process of training
them. They had been meeting in his home, and I am
sure they heard about the raising of the Shunammite's
son, and so they all crowded into his living room
to hear the story. They sat listening to Elisha until
suppertime, and then Elisha asked one of the young
prophets to prepare the food for everyone. There
was a famine in the land at the time, and many young
prophets and their families to feed, so this young man
went out to see if he could forage and find something
to make the pot of stew stretch to feed everyone. He
discovered some good herbs and some wild gourds.
Although not exactly sure what the gourds were, he
thought they looked edible, so he added them to the
stew. The stew smelled savory, and all the men and
their families came and ate together. Suddenly, in the
middle of the meal, someone realized that that gourd
he had added was poisonous, and one of the prophets
cried out fearfully, "There is death in the pot."
 With the best intentions in the world, the
young prophet made a deadly mistake which could
cause others to suffer and perhaps die. They cried out
to Elisha in their desperation. Elisha did not panic. He
simply asked for flour which he added to the pot. Then
he told the prophets to keep eating, and they did

(which I think is its own miracle). The poisoned soup became a nourishing stew.

Sometimes, we can serve God with the best intentions in the world, but the results of all our effort and attempts bring death rather than life-giving nourishment. We say in perplexity and heartbreak, "How did this ever happen?" The temptation at this point is to assume that God's activity is dependent upon our performance. If we fail, He will be unable to work. However, if we believe that He is in control, and if we know that we belong to Him, we can simply cry out and say,

God can use our mistakes for our good and His glory.

"Oh, dear Lord, Jesus. Can you come and take my mistakes and transform them, so that the mistake is changed into life?"

He can use our mistakes for our good and His glory. That is the beautiful promise of Romans 8:28, "All things work together for good for those who love God and are called according to His purpose."

Early in our marriage, Al and I served as missionaries in Colombia, South America. I was a new missionary struggling with Spanish. One of the most embarrassing moments of my whole life happened when we went to a Tuesday Bible study. The study was all in Spanish, and I was the only native English speaker there. My Spanish was not very good, and I always felt awkward and uncomfortable. In fact, every Tuesday, I prayed Jesus might come and get me so I would not have to go to that Bible study, but He never did. Somehow, I lived through it. One evening after the study, we sat around, and all the women came to talk to me and began to ask me questions. I did not understand exactly what they were asking, but I thought they were wondering if my husband was hard working. So, with a big smile on my face, I said, "Oh yes! He is so hard working." As soon as the words came out of my mouth, I knew something was dreadfully wrong. They gasped and moaned and looked horrified. Finally, one other woman who spoke some English said to me, "Honey, they wanted to know if your husband beats you."

"Oh, no!" I said trying to make it right, but it never did really settle down. I came home devastated, embarrassed, and brokenhearted.

"Jesus, how can you use me? I will never count for you!"

Do you know what? Our God is the Lord over all of our mistakes! Pleasing Him is not by our perfect performance; it is simply in our obedience. Just get up and go, obeying even if you feel like you will die. Jesus looks at our heart and our obedience.

> *Our God is the Lord over all of our mistakes! Pleasing Him is not by our perfect performance; it is simply in our obedience.*

Sometimes we cannot even perform. All we can do is get to a certain situation and simply be there as a witness for God, saying to a non-Christian world and to the enemy of our souls, "I am here out of sheer grit and sheer obedience to Jesus Christ." If we begin to just keep on keeping on, it will enable God to give us courage in our souls and transform us so that life can come even from our mistakes.

Recently, I journeyed back to Latin America, and I found such a freedom in Jesus. I did not have to speak beautiful Spanish. I just had to let Jesus love those women through me and vice versa, and it was healing soul time. Jesus is the Lord of our mistakes.

Miracle Number 2: Lord of our Inadequacies

Jesus is the Lord of our inadequacies. Have you ever felt inadequate? Have you said, "God can't use me. He must need someone else." The next little story is so beautiful and addresses just this fear.

> *Then a man came from Baal Shalisha, and he brought the man of God bread of the first fruits, twenty loaves of barley bread, and newly ripened grain in his knapsack. And he said, "Give it to the people, that they may eat." But his servant said, "What? Shall I set this before one hundred men?"*
>
> *He said again, "Give it to the people that they may eat; for thus says the Lord: 'They shall eat and have some left over.'" So, he set it before them; and they ate and had some left over, according to the word of the Lord (4:42-44).*

Another famine came upon Israel, and a farmer brought the first fruits of his field to Elisha. Out of supreme love for God, he offered the first fruits during a famine. What did that cost him? He was so grateful for the harvest that he brought to the prophet the very best he had and gave it to the prophets. In his excitement, he said, "You can feed the whole group of Seminary students with what I've brought."

Elijah handed the bread to the servant and said, "Could you fix supper with this?"

There were a hundred students to feed, and the servant said, "This will never be enough. This is utterly inadequate for what you are asking. It's ridiculous." Elijah said, "You just prepare it, and God will bless and there will be some left over." This little miracle is the prelude to Jesus feeding the five thousand. Remember Jesus took five small barley loaves and two fish from a little boy who surrendered his lunch. He blessed them; broke them, and then He gave them to the people, and there were leftovers. God does not look on us as inadequate; of course, we are inadequate. He simply looks for a willing heart. He wants us to be all His so that He can take us, break us, bless us, and use our lives to feed the multitude, starting in our own homes.

> *God is not asking us to have it all together. Out of our inadequacies, He can transform us and use our lives to count for Him.*

God is not asking us to have it all together. "All you have to have is me. I'm the one that has it all together, and I am the one that is enough. Out of your inadequacies, I can transform you and use your life to count for me, beginning in that home or that dorm room or that workplace. Out of your life can flow rivers of living water to touch a world for God." That little farmer came in a time of famine and gave the best that he had to God, and God used it to feed a hundred seminarians. Don't you love these miracles? They are miracles of the kitchen and miracles of the pantry, because that is where we live.

There was a young mother who had lots of children and not much money. All the children wore hand-me-downs, and there was nothing new in the house. She was not working outside the home, and she had no money of her own. One week, a missionary came to their church, and the pastor challenged every member of the congregation to contribute to the missions offering. Of course, the pastor meant money, but she had no money to give.

God can take the ordinary and transform it into the supernatural.

She prayed about it and said, "Jesus. I don't have anything I can really give. I only have hand-me-down clothes." Just then she remembered that she had twelve new cloth diapers someone had given to her for the latest baby. She decided to give two of those diapers, so she took them to church and put them in the missionary offering plate. That little missionary went home and found two clean diapers in the offering, and so she tenderly tucked them away in her suitcase. One day, that missionary family was in a new church way out in the jungle. They were serving communion there for the very first time, and she thought, "I wish I had a cloth to put over the communion elements." In a flash, she remembered those two diapers, and she pulled them out and placed them gently and lovingly over the body and blood of Jesus Christ. His presence transformed those ordinary diapers, and they became communion cloths for that brand-new little church.

God wants to do the same with your life and mine. He wants all of us. As we give Him ourselves and everything we own, even clean white diapers, He transforms them and uses them for the kingdom.

We have a God who can do the impossible. He can transform any situation. He can transform our inadequacies and can make us adequate for any situation in which we find ourselves. It is not in us and in our abilities. It is in Him. The secret is getting to know Jesus, so Jesus is the sweetest friend of your heart and mind. He is the God who can take the ordinary and transform it into the supernatural.

Miracle Number 3: Lord of our Accidents

Then comes the next little miracle in the story of Elisha and his small band of prophets.

> And the sons of the prophets said to Elisha, "See now, the place where we dwell with you is too small for us. Please, let us go to the Jordan, and let every man take a beam from there, and let us make there a place where we may dwell."
>
> So, he answered, "Go."
>
> Then one said, "Please consent to go with your servants."
>
> And he answered, "I will go." So, he went with them. And when they came to the Jordan, they cut down trees. But as one was cutting down a tree, the iron ax head fell into the water, and he cried out and said,
>
> "Alas, my master! For it was borrowed." So, the man of God said, "Where did it fall?" And he showed him the place. So, he cut off a stick, and threw it in there; and he made the iron float.

Therefore, he said, "Pick it up for yourself." So he reached out his hand and took it (6:1-7).

The students of Elisha grew so numerous that they needed more dwelling places. They came to Elisha and asked if they could build another place to meet and to sleep. Elisha agreed, and they asked him to come with them. I love the fact that they enjoyed Elisha's presence. They were energetic and industrious disciples. They went down together to the Jordan River to start building the new school. The school was to be a home where they could all live together, study together, and work together in order to know God. Then they would go out and share with others what they learned from him. As they met by the side of the Jordan, cutting and stacking trees, the head of one of axes fell into the water. The prophets reached for it, but it sunk to the bottom of the Jordan, and the man who was using it looked up in despair at Elisha and said, "Oh Master, it is borrowed. What shall I do?" Again, we see the love and calmness of Elisha. He took a stick and threw it into the water, and the iron axe head floated to the surface. The man scooped it out of the water, and it was restored.

Our God is the Lord over the accidents that occur in your life and in my life. If you love Jesus, you will find that there will be accidents in life. You will be stricken with how life can change in a few moments. The questions become,

"What do I do now and how do how do I get over this? I am completely out of control and afraid."

Remember the story of Joni Erickson Tada who went swimming as a teenager and dove in rocky water. She hit her head and became a quadriplegic for life. She found herself strapped to a frame inside a hospital, and she could not even move her hands and arms to kill herself. Finally, she said, "Oh God. If you cannot give me grace to die, will you give me a way to live? I give you all that I am—even as a quadriplegic. Please make a way for me to live. If you don't heal me, give me grace to live with victory in a wheelchair." God took that accident and her surrender and made her one of the clearest witnesses of what God can do in a life that is completely committed to Him. She began a ministry for paralytics and quadriplegics and handicapped people and then for the unborn. God can take our accidents and use them to transform His world. As we give to Him the accidents that occur in life, Jesus can take our pain and transform it for our good and for His glory in the redemption of people whom we have never even met.[10]

> *Jesus can take our pain and transform it for our good and for His glory in the redemption of people whom we have never even met.*

The sweetest present you could give to Jesus is yourself—with all your imperfections, failures, and inadequacies—and let Jesus work in your life the amazing miracles of transformation and provision and grace. Then, He can use your life to be His instrument in defeating the enemy and drawing others into His love.

Miracle-Working God

These three mini-miracles point to the larger miracle that God works in 2 Kings 6. Our God not only has authority over mistakes, inadequacies, and accidents, He has authority over all worldy powers. In this next chapter, the Lord outsmarted all His enemies and saved His people:

> *Now the king of Syria was making war against Israel; and he consulted with his servants, saying, "My camp will be in such and such a place." And the man of God sent to the king of Israel, saying, "Beware that you do not pass this place, for the Syrians are coming down there." Then the king of Israel sent someone to the place of which the man of God had told him.*
>
> *Thus, he warned him, and he was watchful there, not just once or twice. Therefore, the heart of the king of Syria was greatly troubled by this thing; and he called his servants and said to them, "Will you not show me which of us is for the king of Israel?" And one of his servants said, "None, my lord, O king, but Elisha, the prophet who is in Israel tells the king of Israel the words that you speak in your bedroom."*
>
> *So, he said, "Go and see where he is, that I may send and get him." and it was told him, saying, "Surely, he is in Dothan." Therefore, he sent horses and chariots and a great army there, and they came by night and surrounded the city. And when the servant of the man of God arose early and went out, there was an army, surrounding the city with horses and chariots. And his servant said to him, "Alas, my master! What shall we do?"*

So, he answered, "Do not fear, for those who are with us are more than those who are with them." And Elisha prayed, and said, "Lord, I pray, open his eyes that he may see."

Then the Lord opened the eyes of the young man, and he saw. And behold the mountain was full of horses and chariots of fire all around Elisha. So, when the Syrians came down to him, Elisha prayed to the Lord and said, "Strike this people, I pray, with blindness." And He struck them with blindness according to the word of Elisha.

Now Elisha said to them, "This is not the way, nor is this the city. Follow me, and I will bring you to the man whom you seek." But he led them to Samaria.

So it was, when they had come to Samaria, that Elisha said, "Lord, open the eyes of these men, that they may see." And the Lord opened their eyes, and they saw, and there they were, inside Samaria!

Now when the king of Israel saw them, he said to Elisha, "My father, shall I kill them? Shall I kill them?"

But he answered, "You shall not kill them. Would you kill those whom you have taken captive with your sword and your bow? Set food and water before them, that they may eat and drink and go to their master."

Then he prepared a great feast for them; and after they ate and drank, he sent them away and they went to their master. So, the bands of Syrian raiders came no more into the land of Israel (6:8-23).

The first thing that happens when we surrender all to Jesus is that the raiders of the enemy will begin to try to infiltrate our hearts and our homes. The enemy will show up at your door, and you will think, "Wait a minute, I thought I had fought this battle." At different times, the enemy comes back and begins to hassle us and tries to make us lose our peace. We begin to learn how to allow God to fight our battles for us and to bring the victory.

The king of Syria was raiding the people of Israel once again, and he planned his attacks with his military leaders in Damascus. Somehow, wherever he planned to place his army, Israel figured it out and eluded or defeated his army. It happened so many times, the king of Syria started to look around, thinking that he had a traitor in his own inner circle. His advisors said,

We do not have to live defeated but can have the victory over the evil one in our lives.

"Oh no, there is a prophet in Israel who knows the heart of God and knows our plans." The God of Israel told Elisha how the Syrians were going to attack, and Elisha told the king. All the plans of the enemy were foiled, and the raids on the people of God came to nothing. Elijah lived so close to the presence of God that he was able to tell the king where and when the enemy was going to move.

We can begin to live so pressed into the heart of God that when the enemy begins periodic raids on our lives, perhaps depression or financial struggles or attacks on our children, and we want to revert to old ways of thinking and old patterns of life, we actually have the freedom and power to press into God and thwart the plans of the enemy. We can say, "Jesus

Christ's blood has given me power in the name of Jesus to resist this the enemy. I do not have to live defeated but can have the victory over the evil one in my life." We can stand in the name of Jesus against these raids of the enemy in our lives.

When the king of Syria recognized that the informer was coming from inside Israel, he realized that he was no longer fighting against Israel but against Israel's God. At this point, the king of Syria had a choice, to respect the God of Israel and back away or to attempt to fight against Him. The king chose the latter option, and this whole chapter is devoted to the folly of fighting against the Eternal God. Instead of drawing back or falling on his face in worship, the king of Syria hardened his heart, and he went after Elisha himself.

> *We have a choice today. We can come face to face with the reality of God in our lives, or we can harden our hearts.*

We have a choice today. We can come face to face with the reality of God in our lives, or we can harden our hearts. The king of Syria hardened his heart, went against Elisha, and found himself in for a surprise.

My dear friend Jeannine is a missionary in Colombia. She was invited to go into a maximum-security prison to witness. She met a man in prison, who had found Jesus, but he could not read or write. He taught himself to read in prison and after he was released, God called him to go back in and preach to the prisoners. He stood up to preach in this depraved place where there were more than sixty murders a month, and blood spattered the walls and floor. It was quite literally hell on earth, but he obeyed and went in and got permission to preach. The first time he preached to only about thirty prisoners, but the murders began to stop.

Then he went to Jeannine and he said, "Jeannine, I have new believers here. Can you come and start some seminary classes and some Bible studies with me?"

"I am not called to prison ministry," she said.

"But I can't get anyone else to go," he responded. "No one sees the vision of it. Please go with me." Jeannine agreed, and she began to go every week and preach and teach God's word. As they opened up the Scriptures, the men began to find Christ. Then, they asked if they could paint the prison walls and put Scripture verses on them. Then, they began to have all-night prayer meetings, and then they started a seminary right there in the prison. There are more than five hundred men involved in Bible studies in that prison. God is transforming the men behind the walls. There were so many guerillas housed in this prison that the secrets of the drug trade began to be shared with people in authority. One of the new believers came to them and said,

God is the God of the miraculous; He is the God of the transforming power.

"Last night I had a dream, and in the dream there was a stash of arms underneath a certain part of the prison floor, and I believe there's going to be a riot." When they went to check, sure enough, the weapons were stored under the floor. This is exactly what happened with Elisha and the king of Israel.

God is the God of the miraculous; He is the

God of the transforming power; God is the God of Elijah, and He is the same God today. It is folly for you and me to fight against God.

When Elisha's servant woke up and began to prepare for the day, he looked out of the window and saw an army surrounding the entire city. His heart fainted with fear; I am sure he knew that Elisha was involved in some way. He ran to Elisha and said, "Master, master. What am I going to do? What are we going to do? We are utterly defenseless against this army. It's all over for us." The servant was looking at the circumstances instead of at God Himself. We can get so overwhelmed with our circumstances that we cannot see that God is at work and is fighting our battles for us. Just when the servant thought that all was lost, Elisha said, "Oh God, open his eyes that he can see." When the servant looked out the window again, he saw chariots and horses of fire surrounding the Syrian army.

> *We can get so overwhelmed with our circumstances that we cannot see that God is at work and is fighting our battles for us.*

Then Elijah said to him, "Don't worry. There are more with us than there are with our enemy." Does that not sound like the words of Jesus, "Greater is he that is in you than he that is in the world"? We do not have to worry. God is fighting for us. He is going to take care of us. He is going to work for us. Don't look at the circumstances. Look at God!

The servant saw God's army, and ironically the Syrian army lost their sight. God was simply making their inner condition an outer reality. The men who came to arrest Elisha were struck with blindness, and Elisha led the whole army right into the hands of the king of Israel. It was an utter and complete victory for the people of God and not one weapon had been used. God moved in supernaturally as only God can do.

When our circumstances become so overwhelming that all we can see is the disarray and despair, and we find ourselves desperate for God to move, this is the moment that God wants us to see that, "greater are they that are with us than they that are against us."

> *Don't lose heart, dear one! Hold on and look up!*

Have we gotten angry with God because he has not worked the way we wanted him to?

We think, "I have waited so long for you to answer and it's like I'm dialing 9-1-1. The phone rings and rings and rings, and you do not answer me. I am losing heart."

Don't lose heart, dear one! Hold on and look up! The resurrected Lord Jesus will come in His time.

I read a story about a man named Roger who was on leave from the Army, and he was hitchhiking home for the holidays. A great big luxury car pulled up and picked him up; it had beautiful leather seats. Roger slid in and told the man he was headed toward Chicago. "You're in luck," said the man. "I am headed to Chicago too." Roger and the man talked small talk, and then Roger, who was a Christian, felt compelled to share Jesus with this man. He felt afraid because this man seemingly had everything money could buy. He felt hesitant and shy, but the Lord just kept pressing his heart. Before the trip ended, he had told that wealthy businessman all about Jesus, and much to his astonishment the man burst into tears, pulled over to the side of the road and prayed to ask Jesus Christ to come into his life. Then he drove Roger to his door and dropped him off.

Roger did not hear from the man again. He got married, and five years later he happened to be in the town of Hanover where this man's business was. He remembered and decided to go and see him. He went to the man's business and asked for an appointment. The secretary said that there was no way for him to be seen, but would he like to see his wife?

Roger happily agreed and went into her office, "How do you know my husband?" she asked.

"Five years ago, he gave me a ride; we happened to talk about Jesus, and we prayed together, and I just wanted to see my brother in Christ." At that point, the successful business woman put her head down on the desk and began to cry. Then she lifted her face and asked, "What day would that have been?"

"May 7th. I remember because I was headed home from the army."

The wife grew quiet and grave and said, "After he dropped you off, he had a head-on collision, and he died instantly. I had been praying for him since we had gotten married, but I never knew he had responded to receive Christ. I have had no assurance of his salvation, so I said, 'God you failed me. You didn't come through. I am not serving you anymore.'" She let bitterness into her soul, and she walked away from the presence of

> *God is asking us to trust Him even though we cannot see what He is doing.*

God. "I have been living out of His presence all these years and then you come in and tell me how God came through even though I didn't believe Him and even though I didn't hang on in trusting faith." That widow came back to Christ that day because of the witness of Roger.

God is asking us to trust Him even though we cannot see what He is doing. If we hang on even in the dark places and say, "Yes, I believe Jesus. I believe, and I will not let go. I am going to hold on even though I do not see. I believe that the end is not yet here, and I choose to trust you, Jesus, because you are the love of my heart." Even if you are in a dark, dark situation, don't let go! Don't look at the circumstances! Look up! Look at Jesus and then just hold on to Jesus.

> *God asks us to let go of our anger, our hurt, our vindictive spirits, and our fears and trust Him to win the battle in His time and in His way!*

Finally, Elisha brought the Syrians to the king of Israel. The king looked at the prophet (only in Israel would a king ask permission from a prophet) and asked, "Can I kill these marauders who have wreaked havoc on my people?" The response of the king of Israel was justice and revenge, but that was not the way of the God of Israel.

Elisha said, "No, instead, let's feed them dinner and send them safely back home." God does not fight our battles the way we fight them. His warfare tactics are never ours. He loved the Syrians as much as He loved the Israelites. He is a God of justice, but He is a God of mercy too. The king of Israel did what Elisha

CHAPTER 7 – THE THREE MINI-MIRACLES   175

instructed. The soldiers went home with eyes that could see and stomachs that were fed, and they raided Israel no more!

God will bring the victory for us, even if He works in unexpected ways, but if we insist on revenge or vengeance, we will sabotage the purposes of God. God asks us to let go of our anger, our hurt, our vindictive spirits, and our fears and trust Him to win the battle in His time and in His way! He says to us,

"Will you let me take care of them and let me take care of you?

Will you choose to love? Let me love them and forgive them through you? And for you?"

God is the one that comes in power in your life and mine, and instead of bringing violence and death, He brings a fellowship meal.

Only Jesus can do that. That is what Holy Communion is all about. That is what Easter is all about. Jesus, who became the sacrificial lamb and took the sins of the world upon Himself, your sins and my sins, is the One that is trustworthy. Let Him settle the score and let Him move into your heart and my heart with Calvary love, Trinity unity and Jesus' forgiveness.

> *Let Jesus move into your heart and my heart with Calvary love, Trinity unity, and Jesus' forgiveness.*

A missionary couple from Northern Canada went to the Amazon jungle to work with a group of native people. This tribe was a very brutal tribe, and the first three missionaries to go there had been killed.

The husband felt the call to go to these particular people, and when they arrived, they realized that there was a famine and this people group were dying from starvation. The level of their need caused an openness to this couple, and they began to listen to the stories of the great Chief who had sent his son to die for them that all the wrong things in their hearts might be forgiven. He had taken their sin upon himself so that they might be forgiven. They listened to the missionary tell them that they might know this great Chief and then they might spend eternity with him. As they began to read from the pages of Holy Scripture, the people listened. At Christmas time, the couple was feeling a bit discouraged because although they listened, the people had not opened their hearts to Christ. They felt the darkness was too great, so they sat down to their Christmas dinner of turtle and sweet potatoes with heavy hearts. A man called outside their tent and handed them a newborn baby. Forcefully, he said, "Take this baby and let it live." The mother had died in childbirth, and they always buried the baby with the dead mother. In their heart of hearts, this young couple knew that God was beginning to break through the darkness and shine His light into that tribe.

The neighboring tribe came and fought against that tribe until there were few warriors left. The missionaries began to pray and said, "Oh God, can you stop the revenge and this culture of death?" Soon, the son of the chief went out of the jungle and caught

The sweetest present we can give to Jesus is ourselves— with all our imperfections, failures, and inadequacies.

the flu. He became very ill and returned to his people to die there. Walking through the jungle, he encountered a warrior from the opposing tribe. Before the opposing man could spear him, the chief's son spoke up and said, "I'm getting ready to die, but there are some people in our village and they're reading pages from a book. Listen to me and let me tell you about those pages from the black book." And so, he began to tell this other man about the God of gods who came down in love to save His people.

The next day someone said to the missionary, "Some of the opposing enemy is in our village. We need you to come—can you come and talk to them? They want to see the book, and they want you to read the white pages to them." The chief's son lived, and God began to change a culture from one of vengeance and death to one of forgiveness and life.

Is there death in our hearts? Or do we know the life-giving freedom of Jesus' blood that was shed for us?

He can use our lives to be His instrument in defeating the enemy and drawing others into His love.

That is what Calvary is all about. He wants to take the vengeance and the unforgiveness and the rage in us and replace it with Himself. He wants us to put our weapons down. We are no more able than the king of Syria or the servant or Elijah himself to surrender our rights and let God take care of us, but the Holy Spirit can do it in us if we will let Him. That is what humility is. We are not arrogant. We receive His love and His care in our lives!

Personal Reflection

Do you ever feel like all you make are mistakes? Do you ever feel discouraged by the accidents or inadequacies in your life? God wants to redeem every part of our lives, even when we don't get it right. If our lives are surrendered to Him, He can use anything we offer to Him—even the mess ups. Spend some time with Him. Commit into His hands all that you do not understand or cannot make right.

When we allow Jesus full lordship in our lives, He not only transforms our mistakes, He writes our story in His eternal story. When the battles come, we find the King of kings fighting for us and for His glory. Do you know the joy of this life with Jesus?

Notes

Notes

CHAPTER
8

IN TIMES OF FAMINE

Many stories in Scripture surprise me by their morbid tone and explicit details. The Bible was certainly not written by a mother wanting to protect her children. This next story in the drama of Elijah and Elisha is one of those. Shock and horror are mingled with amazement at the miracles of God during a national disaster. The famine was so severe in the land of Israel at this time that a donkey's head sold for eighty shekels (the people of God were not even allowed to eat a donkey's head). The Syrians had come and once again were besieging the people of God. There was intense suffering among the people of God inside the wall of Jerusalem, and they were surrounded; no water or food could come in or go out of the city. The writer of the book of Kings sets the stage for us with graphic and horrifying details. He describes the cannibalism to which the people of God had been reduced: mothers eating their babies.

> Then as the king of Israel was passing by on the wall, a woman cried out to him saying, "Help, my Lord, O King!"
>
> And he said, "If the Lord does not help you where can I find help for you? From the threshing floor, from the winepress?" Then the king said to her, "What is troubling you?"
>
> And she answered, "This woman said to me, 'Give your son, that we may eat him today, and we will eat my son tomorrow.' So we boiled my

son, and ate him and I said to her on the next day, 'Give your son that we may eat him, but she had hidden her son'" (6:26-30).

If there was ever a chapter that dealt with depravity and distress, this is the chapter.

It may be that we as a people of God in the 21st century in the United States of America are at about the same point of spiritual famine in our lives. Our society is in chaos because it has turned against truth and against the One who brings life. No longer can God be in public schools and no longer can we pray in public. We have rejected all truth, and now we are in chaos in our educational system. We have rejected God's truth and live in confusion about gender, sexuality, and family as well as issues of right and wrong, good and evil. We are in chaos as a culture. We have walked away from the eternal God, and we are as apostate today as they were then.

We may not be experiencing the physical famine to the degree that the children of God were in their day, but we are experiencing emotional, psychological, mental, and spiritual need in a dimension that we have never known before. We even know an economic or emotional cannibalism that preys on another person so that our own needs are met; we live in a cultural atmosphere rife with that attitude. Finding personal fulfillment, no matter who pays the price, seems to have become the "American Way." That is

> *Our society is in chaos because it has turned against truth and against the One who brings life.*

why we have killed millions of unborn babies; we do not want to be inconvenienced. As a culture, we are looking for self-fulfillment more than any other thing. Jesus says to us, "Why don't you seek a relationship with me first and let me take care of your needs?"

The women did not seek God; instead, they had incredible needs and tried to meet them in their own way, and catastrophe resulted—as it always does when we try to meet our own needs. The king saw the depravity of his people, and he cried out and covered himself with sackcloth, but he did not turn to God. In fact, he blamed all the wretchedness on the prophet of the living God. He said, "I want to get rid of the prophet of God. It's all his fault." The king who could have cried out to God chose to turn away from Him. He did not repent, nor did he ask God for help; instead he fumed against the One who could help him:

> *Jesus says to us, Why don't you seek a relationship with me first and let me take care of your needs.*

> Now it happened when the king heard the words of the woman that he tore his clothes; and as he passed by on the wall, the people looked and there underneath he had sackcloth on his body. Then he said, "God do more to me do to me and more also, if the head of Elisha the son of Shaphat remains on him today!" (6:31).

Are there any unmet needs is your life? Of course there are!

Are you seeking personal self-fulfillment at any cost?

Is God calling you and me to repentance?

Are we like the king, knowing that God has allowed circumstances to get our attention but refusing to cry out to him and repent?

It must be somebody else's fault. We find a scapegoat and blame someone else. We refuse to repent as the King of Israel did.

Elisha knows the cause of Israel's trouble, but he has a much different perspective than the king. The king sends his messenger to Elisha and his group of prophets:

> *Then Elisha said, "Hear the word of the Lord. Thus, says the Lord, 'Tomorrow about this time a seah of fine flour shall be sold for a shekel and two seahs of barley for a shekel at the Gate of Samaria.'"*
>
> *So, an officer on whose hand the king leaned answered the man of God, and he said, "Look if the Lord would make windows in heaven, could this thing be?"*
>
> *And he said, "In fact, you shall see it with your eyes, but you will not eat of it" (7:1-2).*

Down through the ages, God has had a remnant, a few who have gotten to know Him, a few who have entered the dimension of knowing God, not just knowing about Him but knowing Jesus for who He is and falling irrevocably in love with Him. These few entered a personal love relationship with the Eternal

God, and God was no longer an object or a plaything that they manipulated or used, but a Friend, a Savior, a Beloved. God helped these few comprehend, see, understand, and know that God loves them and has given Himself for them that they could know Him and could love Him in return. There is a line that marches down through the ages of human history; we can trace it all the way back from the beginning of those that have known God and walked with God, for whom Jesus Christ has been the love of their souls. These have persevered to the end and have called others to Christ. It is possible to live in daily fellowship with Him.

It is possible to live in daily fellowship with Jesus.

Like the disciples of Elisha, we sit at the feet of Jesus and wait for Him for direction and help. We must do exactly what the prophets did in this chapter: make a circle around Jesus and sit as close to Him as possible.

I remember one time being so confused about what I was supposed to do that I ran into someone's house who loved Jesus with all her heart and just stood there in the foyer. She was not even home; I was simply dropping something off, but as I stood there, the confusion vanished. Suddenly, God was there, and He said, "Beth, this is what you are supposed to do." I do not even remember what He told me, simply the sense of His immediate and comforting presence.

As believers, we come together sitting at the Prophet's feet, only it is not Elisha but Jesus Himself. "Jesus, we want to be as close to you as we can. We want to get as near to you as it is possible to be. Jesus, would you let us see what you want us to see today about yourself?"

There is a difference in coming to Jesus for something and coming to Him because you love Him and would rather be with Him than anyone else in the world. The essence of holiness is when there is no division between my inner life and my outer works. When my actions are motivated by a deep, personal and abiding love for Jesus, then He is free to live and love through me. There is no way you and I can keep the Ten Commandments. There is no way we can keep the Beatitudes. There is no way we can even love our families the way we are supposed to unless we fall in love with Jesus Christ, and He comes and lives His life out in us.

> *When my actions are motivated by a deep, personal and abiding love for Jesus, then He is free to live and love through me.*

When my son Billy was a senior in high school, my husband took him camping and trail riding in the Smoky Mountains. I was home alone, and as I prayed Jesus began to talk to me about how I had lost my first love for Him in the busyness of life. I didn't really see it right at first, but He had an object lesson to help me learn. We had been storing some furniture for missionary friends, and they returned to the states and needed to retrieve all the pieces we had been keeping for them. By the time they finished taking all that belonged to them, my house was in an utter mess. Dressers were emptied out, and stuff seemed to be everywhere. It was as if something had changed in every room of the house, so I began to do a serious house clean. I needed a storage box, so I went in the attic, and the attic was a disaster. I began to clean the attic on Monday, and then that entire week, I went room by room by room and put it all back in order. When Al and Billy returned on the weekend, the house was spic and span and organized. As I worked that week, I began to get so excited because it seemed that Jesus not only wanted to clean out my home but clean out my heart as well.

God wants to get us into His own presence. He is desperately interested in fellowship with us.

During that week, I slept at my parents' house because ours was in such disorder. One night, I got up and my dad was awake, and in the middle of the night we started to talk. It was one of those precious times that God gives in life. He said, "You know, down through the ages, there have been a remnant of people like Abraham, Moses, and Joseph who have really known God, and the closer I get to eternity, the more I sense God is drawing my heart deeper and deeper into Himself. The hunger is growing in my heart for His Word. I want to know Him and to love Him. At this stage of my life, when all the non-essentials are being stripped away, it is as if He is calling me again into His heart, wanting fellowship with me."

He said, "It reminds me a little bit of when I was courting Elsie; I couldn't wait to get her alone. I wanted her all for myself. Do you know what? That's what I feel that Jesus is saying to me. I can't wait to get you all to myself. You are the one I love. I want to have fellowship with you."

God wants to get us into His own presence. He is the love of our hearts, and He is desperately interested in fellowship with us. "I am the One that died for you, I am the resurrection blessing. I want to get you alone, and sometimes I allow the famine to finally get your attention."

That night in the kitchen, my father went on to say that often at the end of a life lived in love with Jesus Christ, there is a stripping away. Amy Carmichael, the great missionary to children in India, found herself shut up as an invalid for the last twenty years of her life. It is as if Jesus draws the loved one into His own embrace, into His own presence, and a great fruitfulness comes simply out of that intimacy and love relationship. In those twenty years, Amy wrote as she lay in her bed: *Edges of His Ways*, *Rose from Briar*, and *Gold by Moonlight*, books that I have read and reread because the Lover drew the beloved to Himself.

We have good news. The answer is not in Christian ministry. The answer is not in revival. The answer is not in working for Jesus. The answer is a love relationship with Jesus Himself through His Spirit, where He lives in you and in me, and we love Him with all our being. As we live in intimacy with Him, with nothing held back, He is free to come and live His life out in me.

> *As we live in intimacy with Jesus, with nothing held back, He is free to come and live His life out in us.*

When I live in that love relationship with Jesus Christ through the power of the Holy Spirit, then I do not have to manipulate other people to meet the needs of my own heart. God can meet me, and then I am free to relate to all those God brings into my life.

One day we picked up my daughter from the airport with her three young babies. They had been on the West Coast for several weeks, and the day of travel had been a long and tiring one. I was fretting about those babies (as any good grandmother would do). As I watched them in the airport and in the car on the way home, I realized those children were perfectly content as long as their mommy and daddy were nearby. We had two cars for all the people and luggage, and the little girls kept asking about where each family member was riding. They wanted to make sure that they were all together. When they understood that everyone was going together, they snuggled in and were as happy as could be. It was the personal presence of the ones that they loved and trusted that mattered, not where they were in the country. Circumstances change, but Jesus remains the One who holds my security in His hands. If I am with Him, I am safe. It is the personal presence of His reality in our lives and in our circumstances that will hold us steady, give us courage, and comfort our hearts. He does not change, so my security is in Him because I know Him, I love Him, and I am learning to listen and obey Him. This is the joy of living in a love relationship with Jesus Christ.

It is the personal presence of His reality in our lives and in our circumstances that will hold us steady, give us courage, and comfort our hearts.

Charles Cowman was a successful telegrapher at the turn of the century. He was from a Christian home and had accepted Christ into his life as a child but soon fell away from his faith. When he was twenty-one, he married his high school sweetheart, Lettie, and they were living happily in Chicago. One day, Lettie went to a Christian meeting, and she was converted. She came back and told Charles all about her experience.

"I can't live a Christian life in a telegrapher's office. It is too difficult," he protested. He was not interested in his boyhood faith, but he loved his wife. Eventually, he agreed to go with her to the service, and when he got home that night, he knelt by his couch and recommitted his life to Christ.

The sense of God's goodness and forgiveness were so real that the next day he joyfully went to his work. He desperately wanted to tell someone what God had done in his heart, but he did not know how. He walked around for thirty minutes trying to figure it out. Finally, he just went in and stood by his co-workers' desk and bumbled out his story. He felt like a hopeless failure, but the next morning the man came and said to him, "Cowman, I went home and asked Jesus into my heart last night. Thanks for sharing with me." The two of them started to hold services on Sunday afternoon for the telegraphers who worked on Sunday. God began to move among them, and they started the first Prayer Band; one of the men who was saved was EA Kilbourne. One day Kilbourne caught the streetcar late and arrived late to work. Cowman was the man in charge, and he was angry when Kilbourne arrived late, so he lectured him and humiliated him. Afterwards, Cowman was heartbroken. God had saved seventy-five men, and now the leader of the little band lost his temper because the streetcar was late. Cowman knew he had grieved God, so he went to see a pastor at Moody Church. The pastor looked at him and said, "You need to be sanctified. God can give you a holy heart, so that you do not lose your temper. Give Jesus all of yourself, and you will find that when Cowman has all of Jesus and Jesus has all of Cowman, your temper will clear right up, and you will live clean."

Cowman said, "Yep, that is what I need." In that pastor's office, Charles Cowman died to Charles Cowman. He walked out of that office God's man with a passion for Jesus Christ.

He came home, and he said to Lettie, "God's got all my heart!" And she knew it. There was a new passion and new power in his life, and one of the places most affected was their checkbook. He said, "We've got to share what it is to know Jesus with the whole world. Let's get into an apartment; that will cost less, and we can give what we've got to support an African missionary." They downsized and began supporting an African missionary. They went one night to hear AB Simpson preach; he was the founder of the Christian Missionary Alliance Church. After the message, AB Simpson said, "Now, we are going to take an offering." Lettie watched in horror as her husband put their month's check, his gold watch and her wedding ring in the offering plate. Finally, he said, "Lettie, we have to give ourselves."

There is a new passion and a new power in our lives when we give ourselves to Jesus.

When Charles and Lettie applied to be missionaries, the missions board said that he did not know enough to go, so they sent him to Moody Bible Institute, and he became trained in the Word of

God. One day when they went to church, there was a Japanese man sitting there named Juji Nakada. They began to talk, and Nakada said, "I am a preacher in Japan, and I heard that a person could come here and find out how to be filled with the Holy Spirit. I want to be filled with the Holy Spirit."

Charles said, "I can tell you how." He did, and the two of them became close friends, and God began to call Charles and Lettie to Japan.

The men from the telegrapher's office were the ones who supported the Cowmans as they headed to Japan. They started a Jesus Doctrine Mission Hall on a main street. Charles and Lettie headed to Japan with $300 for the boat ticket and $240 for the first month's rent for the Mission Hall. They lived in a little house over the preaching Hall, and the only paint they had to paint the walls was red. They had red walls and red ceilings on their three rooms, but Jesus was there. They never went into debt, even though one time they had nothing to serve the visiting bishop except bread and warm tea. God began to move in their souls, and his people got saved. They started a Bible Institute with evangelistic preaching in the morning and a holiness meeting in the afternoon. They wanted their people to know God in all His fullness.

Eventually, the vision came to get a portion of the Scripture into every home in Japan. With Japanese workers and other missionaries, they went door-to-door and covered Japan with the gospel portion. At the end of that evangelistic outreach, Charles was very ill. He had to go home to California and live in a little bungalow, and for six years the two were shut in alone with God. He was so ill that he could not even take a walk around the block without going into heart distress. During the incredible physical trauma of those six years, they also experienced a spiritual trauma. They both believed that God would heal him if they had enough faith. Mrs. Lettie Cowman began searching her soul to try and understand why God was not healing her beloved husband and co-worker for Christ. Out of her soul distress, she put together the devotional, *Streams in the Desert*. It has been re-published more times than we can count, and it may be that their greatest ministry came out of those six years of distress. Then God took Charles home to heaven but continued to use Lettie in a powerful way in world missions.[8]

One couple fell in love with Jesus, and He was given a right to everything they were, everything they possessed, everything they hoped and dreamed of accomplishing with Him. Out of that incredible love relationship came a blessing for all of Japan and then all the Christian world.

What does Jesus want to do today in you? What does he want to do in me?

> *I don't have to worry about where I'm going or what I'm doing. All I have to do is follow my Shepherd.*

If you and I would begin to fall in love with Jesus Christ to the depths of our being and say, "No matter what it costs, I want to be all His. I don't have to worry about where I'm going or what I'm doing. All I have to do is follow my Shepherd," our lives would be transformed.

I have a picture of a little shepherdess in my kitchen and it reminds me every day that all I have to do is follow my Shepherd. He knows where to lead me, and it is safe to trust Him. It is possible to live with heaven in our souls, and adversities, financial trials, and traumas can become the sweetest opportunities in our lives because every one of them points us to Him. Then we go to Him and say, "Jesus, what do I do now?"

Adversities, trials, and traumas can become the sweetest opportunities in our lives because every one of them points us to Him. Then we go to Him and say, Jesus, what do I do now?

During famine, Elisha and his little band sought the Lord, and when God was ready to act, the Word of the Lord came to Elisha. Elisha shared that word with the king. God gave His witness to the king of Israel, and then He moved to free His people from the tyranny and torture of the Syrians. The messenger of the king did not believe Elisha's word, and Elisha promised that athough he would see God's provision, he would never taste it. This is exactly how the unusual story unfolded.

Two lepers who sat by the gate of Israel said to themselves, "Let's go to the Syrian camp and see if they will feed us. The worst thing that could happen is that we would be killed." They went, and they found the Syrian camp had been deserted. All the food and supplies were still in the tents, but there were no soldiers. The lepers feasted on the spoils, and then they returned to Israel to tell them the good news:

> Then they said to one another, "We are not doing right. This day is a day of good news,

and we remain silent. If we went until morning light, some punishment will come upon us. Now, therefore come, let us go and tell the king's household." So, they went and called to the gatekeepers of the city, and told them, saying, "We went to the Syrian camp, and surprisingly no one was there, not a human sound—only horses and donkeys tied and the tents intact." And the gatekeepers called out, and they told it to the king's household inside (7:9-11).

The king did not believe and thought that the Syrians had set a trap, but when he sent messengers to see, they reported that the Syrian camp was deserted. The messenger of the king who had doubted the word of Elisha was trampled in the gate of Israel as everyone raced to the Syrian camp for food and water:

Now the king had appointed the officer on whose hand he leaned to have charge of the gate. But the people trampled him in the gate, and he died, just as the man of God had said, who spoke when the king came down to him. So, it happened just as the man of God had spoken to the king, saying, "Two seahs of barley for a shekel, and a seah of fine flour for a shekel shall be sold tomorrow about this time in the gate of Samaria."

Then that officer had answered the man of God and said, "Now, look, if the Lord would make windows in heaven could such a thing be?" And he said, "In fact, you shall see it with your eyes, but you shall not eat of it. And so it happened to him, for the people trampled him in the gate, and he died" (7:17-20).

Those who listened to the voice of the prophet and believed ate the bread of the Syrians; those who did not believe did not live to participate in the feast God had prepared.

The King of kings confronted the king of Israel through the prophet Elisha; God works to draw everyone to Himself, and He uses many unlikely circumstances to do so. God's word to Elisha was the truth, and Elisha foretold that reality to the king and his court. When we allow the Spirit of Jesus to fill our lives with His presence and His goodness, we find that He uses our lives in unexpected and eternal ways. It is often not what we dreamed or even could imagine, but He writes our stories with a God-sized plot and life-giving word for others.

> *When we allow the Spirit of Jesus to fill our lives with His presence and His goodness, we find that He uses our lives in unexpected and eternal ways.*

Personal Reflection

What are the unmet needs in your life? Are you seeking to meet your own needs instead of bringing them to Jesus Christ? Is God calling you and me to repentance?

When all seems impossible, are we listening to the voice of Jesus, trusting Him for direction through the darkest times? If we do, we will find that He makes a way where there is no way. Are you trusting Him?

Sometimes He answers our prayers in the most surprising and unexpected ways. Are we looking for His answers, no matter what they are? How has He surprised you with His goodness?

Notes

Notes

CHAPTER
9
VICTORY

CHAPTER 9 — VICTORY

The stories of Elijah and Elisha are coming to an end. I always wish there were more stories of these two men of faith. One of the last stories about Elisha is also about our little Shunammite woman, the wealthy woman who made a prophet's chamber for Elisha, to whom Elisha promised a son and whose son Elisha raised from the dead. She appears again. Elisha had warned her that a famine was coming (doesn't it always seem like there is a famine?). God's judgment had come on the Northern Kingdom, and He was trying to get the attention of Judah as well. She listened to Elisha's counsel and went to live in the Philistine country, but when the famine was over, she returned, bringing her son and her household with her. When she returned to Israel, she went to the king to request that her lands and her family home be returned to her.

The Shunammite Woman's Faith

This woman faithfully and consistently followed Yahweh; she trusted Him, provided for His prophet, listened to His counsel and sought Him in her pain. She came to the king in need, and God provided for her, just as she had provided for Elisha. Perhaps the heart of the king was softening towards the Lord, and so he had asked Elisha's servant about the miracles of Elisha. As the servant recounted the story of the little boy whom Elisha raised from the dead, the Shunammite woman and her son appeared in the king's court, to request from the king her property. The servant looked up in surprise and told the king, "For goodness' sake, this is the woman, and this is the son Elisha raised from the dead."

The king was amazed, the servant was amazed, and I am sure that the woman was amazed at the precise timing of God. The king looked at her and at her son and said to a servant, "Give back everything that belongs to her and all that has been produced on the land since she has been away. Restore to her everything."

The enemy of our souls would like us to believe that God will not take care of His people, that He will not meet our needs or be enough for us. He comes and says, "Don't be quite so passionate for Jesus Christ. Don't love Jesus Christ quite so much! Don't love Him with all your heart! Just try to be normal!" The story of the Shunammite is a promise that God will take care of His own. She opened her home and provided for the prophet, and God took care of all her needs to the end of her life. We can trust Him to do the same for us if we will ask Him, trust Him, and obey Him.

> *We can trust God to take care of all our needs if we will ask Him, trust Him, and obey Him.*

The King's Lack of Faith

Chapter 13 gives the story about a man who did not do quite so well as our Shunammite woman. Elisha was sick; he would not be taken directly to heaven like Elijah. He was sick with the illness with which he was to die. He was in a weak physical condition, but not a weak spiritual condition. The king of Israel, whose name was Joash, came to see Elisha weeping. Joash cried over the nation and what would happen to it after Elisha was dead. He mourned for himself as well. Elisha had been a source of security for the entire nation, and the king began to grieve his passing. Joash was afraid of a future without Elisha.

How often does this happen in our lives?

If we allow anything or anyone to become our security but God Himself, we find that we are battling insecurity and fear continually. God alone is big enough and constant enough to be our anchor in the storm and the cornerstone of our lives. Elisha had been that for Joash, and Joash was afraid at the thought of losing him. There is a redemptive weeping that leads to repentance and confession of sin and to a life of obedience and righteousness. There is also a weeping of self-pity because we are afraid and are not getting our own way. The latter, I believe, was the type of tears Joash cried. He wept out of his own self-interest.

God alone is big enough and constant enough to be our anchor in the storm and the cornerstone of our lives.

Elisha had very little patience with the king. He knew the way to victory, and he was willing to show it to King Joash if Joash would cooperate and learn. Elisha was trying to get Joash ready to face life without the prophet's presence in it. He was trying to help him to trust God enough to fight the battles himself. God puts key people in our lives to mentor us, to challenge us in our walks with Christ. They are blessings and gifts from Him, but they are not to replace Him in our lives. Only Jesus Christ can be the perfection, fulfillment, and hope that we are longing to know.

There is victory for the Christian, even when we lose some of our support; Jesus' blood was shed so that we could have all victory in the name of Jesus. Like Elisha with Joash, God is trying to grow us up so that we can hear His voice, we can understand His guidance, and we can walk the distance with Him. The only one that can

> *If we have Jesus we can live in victory.*

go with you and with me is Jesus himself, and if we have Jesus we can live in victory.

The Call to Battle

The first thing that Elisha says to Joash is that there will be a war. The reality is that people who call on the name of the one true God will live in a battle zone. When Jesus called His disciples and sent them out two by two, He let them know that they were going out into a battle:

> *Behold I send you out as sheep in the midst of wolves. Therefore, be wise as serpents and harmless as doves. But beware of men, for they will deliver you up to councils and scourge you in their synagogues. You will be brought before governors and kings for My sake as a testimony to the Gentiles (Matthew 10:16-18).*

Jesus gave His disciples all power to raise the dead, heal the sick, cast out demons, and preach the gospel, while helping them understand that they would be persecuted and would have to learn to live in tension with the world around them. Jesus does not call us to success. He calls us to tension places politically, culturally, economically, and even religiously. He does not call us to an organization or a committee but to Himself. The only place there does not have to be tension is between your heart and the heart of Jesus. Honestly, there will come tension in every other aspect of your life at one time or another. Jesus is still in control, and He can use those very tensions to draw us to Himself so that out of those tensions we get to know Him better. Out of those struggles, God can use your life and mine to be a redemptive agent to a lost world.

God can use your life and mine to be a redemptive agent to a lost world.

If we are going to walk the walk and live in the word of God and have no tension between the Triune God and our own hearts, we will definitely find ourselves in political and cultural tension with the world around us. If we walk with God, and Jesus Christ is the one we follow, we will find tensions come in all areas of life. These tensions will even come among family members. When we decide to follow Jesus and obey whatever He asks, many times our families do not understand. They criticize and think that we are crazy. They give advice, try to change our minds, and sometimes even cut off relationships. Living with tensions inside our own families can be the most painful thing we have to bear. After a while, we grow weary and come to Jesus and say, "Lord, this is not what I expected. I am having to pay a bigger and a more personal price than I anticipated." At this point, God reminds us of the faith of the Shunammite woman. She kept believing, obeying and trusting, and God met her needs at every turn.

Luke 24 tells the story of the Emmaus Road. The disciples are walking along the road, talking of the crucifixion, and Jesus shows up and begins to walk and talk with them. They do not recognize Him. There will be times in our lives when He will be walking with us, and we will not recognize His presence. He will begin to trust us with *the mystery of the unexplained*. We will not be able to understand or to see what Jesus is doing in our circumstances, and we will lose His presence if we are not very careful!

> *Remember the faith of the Shunammite woman—she kept believing, obeying and trusting, and God met her needs at every turn.*

The disciples were in fulltime service for Jesus, and yet Jesus had allowed things to happen in their lives and in His own life that they could not explain. They did not have categories for the cross. It was never supposed to have happened. He was the King, and yet disaster occurred on that Friday. The disciples were walking and talking about the cross, and then the reports of the empty tomb came. They neither understood nor could they make sense of what was happening. Sometimes there comes a tension in my heart with God, and I say to Him, "Jesus, I want to love you with all my heart, but what in the world are you doing with my life? And with the lives of those I love. This is not how I expected you to work, and I do not understand."

The temptation at this point is to look at other people or organizations or churches and say, "Oh, they are not doing it right." Or we look in our own hearts for some hidden or unknown sin and say, "Oh, I am not doing it right." He is asking us to look neither to other people or within our own hearts, but to look to Him and say, "Jesus, I don't understand, but I trust you. Will you take care of me when I do not understand?" Instead of becoming a victim of other people's sins or a victim of our own morbid self-consciousness, we can act like a little child who will nestle close in the arms of a beloved parent until the trial or anxiety is gone.

The Mystery of the Unexplained

We can take our disappointment to Him, whether from ministry, from family, or from our own failure. We can let Him speak His peace and His assurance into our lives. God wants to use the very perplexing circumstances in our own lives for His good purposes. As we trust Him with the mystery of the unexplained, we have the joy of coming to know Him in an intimacy beyond any that we have known. The description from the ancient songwriter will fit our story, "Who is that coming up from the wilderness, leaning on her beloved?" (Song of Songs 8:5). We

> *God wants to use the very perplexing circumstances in our own lives for His good purposes.*

walk through the wilderness, but we walk through it with Him, and we come out leaning on His arm and receiving His strength.

I read about a missionary to Japan called Sensei. She was from Dublin, Ireland. One day she was reading through a missionary magazine, and there was an article that described a certain Miss Penrod and her ministry of working with geisha women, legal prostitutes for businessmen, in Japan. The article was a cry for help from Miss Penrod, and Sensei felt that God was calling her to go and work with Miss Penrod in Japan. Her family thought she was crazy, but she persevered, and two years after her call, she left for Japan. Shortly after arriving in Japan, God began to open doors for her to work with Japanese children who had no one to take care of them.

We walk through the wilderness, but we walk through it with Him, and we come out leaning on His arms and receiving His strength.

Many orphan girls eventually became geisha women, and Sensei felt called to care for them before they got into the life of prostitution. As she waited on God, a whole ministry to these children began to unfold. She built Sunshine Home, a place for orphaned children, and it prospered; the Sunshine Home became a place of safety and blessing. It was known throughout the entire community for its care and love for these unwanted children. In 1939, she came home on furlough, and all of a sudden, she felt a burden to go back to Japan. The burden did not go away, so she made her plans, got on a leaky boat and headed off to Japan. When she got back, the whole atmosphere had changed, and she realized that she would not be able to stay long in Japan—war was about to break out. She began to pray desperately and work feverishly to find homes for all her forty-two little children. She went to the church, and God began to move, and forty-one children found homes. Everyone was placed except a beautiful seventeen-year-old girl. She was too old for anyone to want her. Sensei started to pray, and one day a couple showed up at her door. They had come to see if they could adopt a baby. Their daughter, a seventeen-year-old, had died the year before and they were coming to see if God had another baby for them. Sensei told them that she needed a home for a seventeen-year-old girl, but the couple refused. It would be too heartbreaking.

Sensei prayed, and she went into the kitchen and found the Japanese girl and said, "Would you please serve tea for our guests?" She did a lovely job, and after tea the couple said, "Could you tell us her name and her birthday?" The girl's birthday was the same as the daughter who had gone to heaven the year before, and the couple felt this was God's will for them, and they adopted her with joy. In a matter of days, Sensei was forced to leave the country, but God had provided for all her children: every one of them was in a Japanese Christian home before the war broke out. The burden on Sensei's heart was simply a reflection of the burden on God's heart.[12]

Sometimes the mysterious circumstances in your life and my life mean that Jesus is trying to get a willing vessel to work with Him and for Him, even if we don't understand all the reasons. Sensei did not know all the reasons that God was moving and putting burdens on her heart, but she willingly walked in a love relationship with Jesus Christ so that she heard His voice and trusted in His providence. She believed that God could get her into the right place at the right time to accomplish His redemptive purposes.

Proverbs 4:12 was Sensei's life verse, "As thou goest, step by step, I will open the way." Exodus 23:24 reflects that same theme, "I will send my angel ahead of you to guard you and to bring you to the place or places that I have prepared." As we go forward, our only concern needs to be,

> *Sometimes the mysterious circumstances in your life and my life mean that Jesus is trying to get a willing vessel to work with Him and for Him.*

Are we walking in a love relationship with Jesus, following His lead and listening to His voice?

Are we willing to do this even if there is tension?

Are we willing to do this even if we are trusted with the unexplained?

The king of Israel did not have the courage to trust absolutely. Elisha instructed him to take the bows and arrows. If you and I want to go through with God and on to victory, we will have to live with our weapons in our hands, the weapons of God's warfare, which are the Word of God and the Sword of the Spirit. We must recognize that we are in a battle, and we must always be ready to fight, not in our own strength but in His. Not with our own weapons but with His. Like the children in Narnia with the gifts given by Father

Christmas, we must always bear our weapons and be ready for the battle whenever it comes.

First, we must have the intention to fight the enemy. Elisha told Joash to put his hand on the bow. He placed his hand on top of the hand of the king of Israel. Just like Elisha did for Joash, so Jesus does for us. As we go forward with the intent to follow Christ wholeheartedly and fight the battles that come, God's divine and faithful presence is there to meet us before we ever take a step. God Himself goes with us, and in His name, there is power to resist the enemy in the name of Jesus.

Then Elisha says to Joash, "Open the window." We must be willing to face the enemy that is coming; we must not run away or hide. Our tendency, whenever we face difficult circumstances, is to retreat and cower in fear, but Jesus wants us to open the window and face what is coming. He is the healer. He is the sanctifier. He is the provider. As we face the enemy, we also open our own souls to God for His comfort, strength, and provision. As we face the enemy, we find the strength and help of God to go forward, and it may be

As we face the enemy, we find the strength and help of God to go forward.

that the most important thing we ever do is open the window and face the enemy.

Sometimes in our family, with our own spouses and children, we find the enemy wanting to come in and destroy. We push each other's buttons and find ourselves quarrelsome, grumpy, and unkind. In those moments, Jesus wants us to stop, lift our face to Him and say, "Wait a minute. I am going to open the east window. In fact, I am going to open every window in this house. Let the wind of your Holy Spirit blow in and through this home. Heal us! Set us free! Love through us!" We can claim the freedom that only Jesus can give.

There may be tensions in our churches, but we can open the east window and ask, "Father, how do I have Godly responses to these people? What do I do next? How can you use this in my life for my good and your glory and for the life of the church?"

> *Heal us!*
> *Set us free!*
> *Love through us!*

Open the window and say, "Lord, I do not understand, but I choose you. Would you come in and take my weakness; lead me into obedience and faith." There can come a fullness in your life and mine because God can move in and use us in ways we never dreamed of because He has full control.

Then Elisha commanded Joash to shoot, and he shot the arrow out the window. He obeyed. Whatever God is asking you to do, do it. Put feet to what He is saying to your heart.

Do you need to ask for forgiveness?

Do you need to write a letter of restitution before you go out to the front line?

Do you need to go home and tell your husband you are so sorry you've sinned against him?

Do you need to apologize to your kids?

Do you need to make a phone call and go visit a neighbor?

Do you need to talk to someone about Jesus?

Is there somebody God has laid on your heart for weeks?

What about saying, "God, I am opening that east window. I have wanted to talk to that woman for years, and I've never done it, Lord. I'm going to do it today. I'm going to shoot my bow and arrow just like Joash."

Begin to obey. If we perish, we perish, but we will perish obeying, and I have never known anyone who has perished because of their obedience. God is calling us to absolute and complete obedience.

God wants us to say to Him, I am not letting you go until this circumstance turns around, until this problem in my life is redeemed, until this situation in my life that needs healing is healed.

Then Elisha said, "Take your arrows and strike them on the ground," and so the king of Israel took an arrow and struck the ground three times.

Elisha was impatient and frustrated. "No! You will only have victory over the Syrians three times. You should have struck the ground repeatedly." God wants us to fight our battles until the enemy is completely defeated, not partially or halfway defeated. I am sure the king felt a little silly, and so do we when we keep fighting the enemy—over and over again. God wants us to claim His victory, total and complete. He wants us to say to Him, "I am not letting you go until this circumstance turns around, until this problem in my life is redeemed, until this situation in my life that needs healing is healed. I respond poorly every time, and I am fed up. I am going to go on beating my arrows in prayer until you come and set me free."

This week I had a disaster day. Everything seemed to go wrong, and I thought to myself, "No way! This is the enemy, and I am going to pick up my arrows and claim the complete and full victory of Jesus over the evil one!" I claimed the blood of Jesus over my whole family and over every circumstance. I am believing God for miracles. I am believing that the things that have kept us in bondage, the lies that have kept us from moving on into victory, and the hindrances that have kept us from obedience can be defeated in Jesus' name and by His blood. We do not have to live in defeat. The victory is available. It is our choice if we choose to be victorious and not hold back.

The Shunammite woman did not hold back. She went all the way, and she found her place in Holy Scripture because of her obedience. She is a testimony in a dark land, in a dark hour—one woman who went through with God.

Will you and I hear the heartbeat of Jesus Christ and fall so passionately in love with Him that we will hold on for His full purposes, no matter how long it takes and no matter how much it costs?

I am holding on for the will of God to be accomplished not only in my own life, but in the lives of those I love and the lives of those for whom He has given me responsibility. The enemy cannot have all the homes and families, all the marriages and all the neighborhoods. I am standing in the gap for those around me, taking the arrows given to me and saying, "No, in the name of Jesus. The evil one cannot have his way with these."

The king of Israel did not do that. He hit the ground three times, but he did not hold on for a full victory. Israel did have victory for a while, but then the nation of Israel was assimilated into the culture around them, and the people of God were lost.

Elisha was different. He had said "yes" to God many years ago when he burned his yoke, slaughtered his oxen, turned his back on his old way of life, and followed after the prophet of God.

He stood up to family tension, political tension, and social tension. He lived in utter faithfulness to the God who had called him. Even after Elisha's death, there was enough life and power in his bones to cause a man to receive new life. When the Moabite raiders interrupted the burial of a man who had died in Israel, they quickly put him in the tomb where Elisha's bones were buried. As soon as the body of the dead man touched the bones of Elisha, life was restored, and the man walked out of the tomb. (Probably scaring the living daylights out of the raiders and his friends and family). Elisha's life, by the power of the Spirit of God, became a life of exploding power even after death, (2 Kings 13:20-23).

When we give our lives to Christ and live in the fullness of His Spirit, there comes a power in our lives to live in the presence of God Himself.

When we give our lives to Christ and live in the fullness of His Spirit, there comes a power in our lives to live in the presence of God Himself. His life, His power, His love, and His grace begin to flow out of our lives, and the dead bones of those around us find new life because of His life in us. Like Deuteronomy 6:4, the secret is knowing Him and loving Him and following Him.

Can you willingly trust Him with the tension of following Him and yet live with no tension between His heart and yours?

Are you willing to trust Him with the unexplained?

Are you willing to hold on, believing Him for complete victory in your own life and in the lives of the people you love?

At the shore of the Red Sea, when the Israelites realized the Egyptians were close behind them, they began to panic. In that moment, God came and said to Moses, "The Egyptians you see today, you will never see again" (Exodus 14:13). It was true in Moses' day, and it can be true in our day as we hold on for the victory of God for His people and for His world.

God wants us to claim some battles and some people for Him. There are things for which we must believe Him—some battles that need to be conquered and closed, never to be opened again so that we can move into a new realm of knowing Him and His faithfulness in our lives.

Jesus, as we get ready to head to our places of service, let us not get offended in you or in other people. Put in our hearts the incredible joy of believing that everything God allows, He can use for our good and for His glory. He can use this to do something in our hearts to make us more like Himself and more useful to His service.

Personal Reflection

Are you trusting Jesus for His provision at every season in life? If you are facing a new transition, can you trust Jesus just like the Shunammite woman trusted? He provided for her in marvelous ways. Ask Him for His care and provision currently in your life.

What about the unexplained? Are you willing to entrust all aspects of life into His loving hand and be content with the answers that He gives or does not give?

Are there places in our lives for which God is asking us to claim a victory? He does not want us to give up! Who is He asking you to carry in prayer and in love?

Notes

Notes

Notes

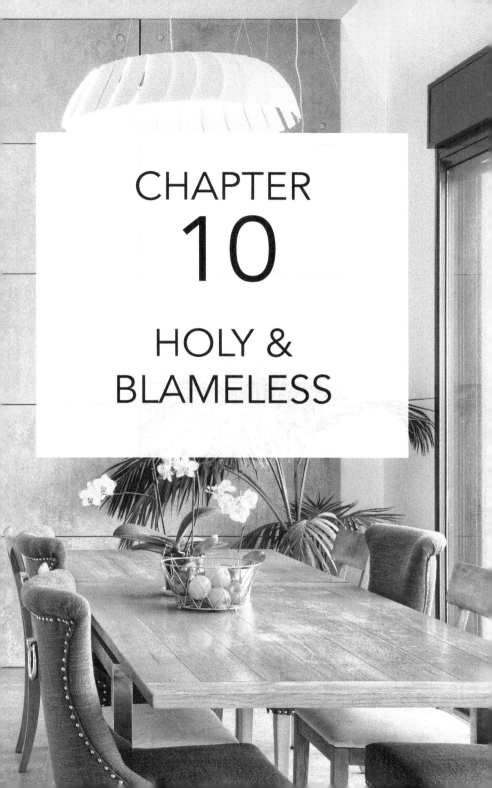

CHAPTER
10

HOLY &
BLAMELESS

While I was getting ready for this series of Bible studies on Elijah and Elisha, my husband and I had a few days of vacation to seek Jesus for the new year. While I was waiting on God, I began to ask Him some serious questions. I had spent weeks studying Elijah and Elisha, and the sobering question had arisen in my mind,

Jesus, how do you get to the place that you can be like an Elijah or Elisha? Filled with the Holy Spirit, powerful and effective in service?

After, I read the story of Elijah and Elisha, I thought a bit incredulously, "Jesus, what can you do with me? I am a homemaker, a mom and a grandmother. I am not in the same category as those men." Elijah and Elisha were men who had blameless hearts. They knew God intimately, and they obeyed Him wholeheartedly. How can I live like they lived? What does it mean to walk before God and be blameless?

All of us can come to the feet of Jesus and be filled with His Spirit, so we can live in wholehearted obedience and unconditional love of Jesus.

In my searching that weekend, God led me to Ephesians to teach me how such a life is possible. Sometimes the Old Testament gives a model that the New Testament explains and makes possible for the ordinary believer. What I learned is that God can make us full of the Spirit of God. This message of the fullness of God's Spirit is for the Jew and Gentile, the rich and poor, the male and female. All of us can come to the feet of Jesus and be filled with His Spirit, so we can live in wholehearted obedience and unconditional love of Jesus.

I want to end our study of the great prophets with the exhortation that the same Spirit who lived in them can indwell our hearts as well. In Ephesians, Paul calls the church to be *"holy and blameless in love"* (Ephesians 1:4). We are adopted into His family, and this adoption is for all men and for all women who will receive Him. He stresses that in 2:8-9,

> *By grace you have been saved through faith, and that is not of yourselves, it is the gift of God....we are His workmanship created in Christ Jesus.*

Salvation is a gift that God gives to us, and we receive it by faith. It is not something that we do. It is not a list or an achievement or good works. It is not our church or prayer meeting attendance—as good as those are. It is not that we follow any lists of dos or don'ts. Our salvation rests completely and freely on the gift given to us in Jesus Christ on the cross. He died for your sins and my sins. He is the only way that any man, woman, or child can get to the Father. Once we enter that love relationship with Jesus Christ, He becomes our peace, and He breaks down that dividing wall of hostility between people, between all of us. He can break down the existential isolation that we feel because He is the Prince of Peace. Once we enter that love relationship and Jesus saves us from our sins, He wants to move into our hearts; He wants to fill us with His Spirit and *"He wants to make us for the praise of His glory"* (Ephesians 1:14). In order to do this, He seals us with His Holy Spirit. We might ask,

Why do I need to be sanctified?

Why do I need to be filled with the Holy Spirit?

That is a great question! We were not created to be complete and independent apart from God. We were created for Him, to be made whole in Him, and the fact that we cannot do this on our own is simply an awareness of our created nature. Sin pushes away and causes rebellion in our spirits; sin makes us want to achieve spiritual success on our own, but we cannot. We were made for Him, and when we receive Him in salvation and sanctification, He enters in, cleanses us and does the work of full salvation. He fills us and empowers us; His Spirit enables us to walk with God and be blameless.

Ephesians is a beautiful book because it gives the theology in some of the most beautiful language in Scripture, and then it moves right into the practicalities of daily living in Christ. I love how God writes the Word. I ask Him for a practical example, and He gives it.

How is holiness lived out in the nitty gritty of daily life?

Walk Worthy

Walk in Love

Walk in the Light

Walk Wisely

He teaches us how to walk before Him and be blameless, and He gives it to us in four steps: Walk Worthy (Ephesians 4:1), Walk in Love (Ephesians 5:1), Walk in the Light (Ephesians 5:8) and Walk Wisely (Ephesians 5:16).

After we have received Christ's offer of salvation, and after we have surrendered completely to Him, we find that the next thing He asks us to do is Walk: to go forward, living in Him, learning to obey Him and loving Him in all that life brings our way. Many times, we think that the essence of Christian life is in spiritual mountaintops, but it is not. As we walk with Christ, we find our relationship with Him and with others deepening, growing, and becoming more beautiful every day. Experiences allow us to enter a love relationship with Jesus Christ Himself, but the *relationship* with Him is our priority. We do not just have two crisis experiences (salvation and sanctification), but we learn to walk with the One we love. This is the reality that Elijah and Elisha understood and practiced.

As we walk with Christ, we find our relationship with Him and with others deepening, growing, becoming more beautiful every day.

As we walk with Him, God wants to free us to love Him and to be able to relate in truth and in joy. The only way we can do this is if we make Him the first love of our hearts and allow Him to be God in our lives. When He is in first place, God begins to bring order and freedom and joy. Depression, despondency, and chaos are not to be our story! We begin to walk in the light and to walk wisely. A singing heart, a thankful heart, and a submissive spirit are the gifts of God's Holy Spirit to us. He gave all of Himself on Calvary to say, "I love you." How much does He love us? With arms wide open, He says to us "I love you this much!"

Elijah and Elisha represent some of Scripture's finest examples of those who walked with God. As they did, they found Him to be more than enough to meet the needs of their own lives, the needs of their communities and the needs of the nation. God used their willing hearts to bring an entire nation back to Himself. I believe He is wanting some women who will say, "Yes, I want to be filled with the Spirit of God so that I may walk worthy, walk in love, walk in the light, and walk wisely just as Elijah and Elisha did in days gone by."

God used their willing hearts to bring an entire nation back to Himself.

May Jesus hear our prayers and fill us with His Holy Spirit.

Notes

Notes

Endnotes

CHAPTER 1. PROVIDENCE UNIVERSITY
1. TenBoom, Corrie, *The Hiding Place*. (NY, Bantam Books, 1974), 20.

CHAPTER 2. ALL OF ME FOR ALL OF HIM
2. Prentiss, Elizabeth, *Steping Heavenward*, (New York, Hurst & Co., 1899), 41.

CHAPTER 3. THE RESTORATION OF GOD
3. Mains, Karen. *Karen, Karen*. (Carol Stream, IL, Tyndale House, 1979), 61.

CHAPTER 4. SQUEAKY CLEAN HEARTS
4. Kuhn, Isobel, *Second Mile People*. (Singapore, OMF, 2008), 86.

5. Taylor, Dr. and Mrs, *Hudson Taylor's Spiritual Secret*. (Grand Rapids: Discovery House, 1990), 92.

CHAPTER 5. PLANNING FUNERALS OR RESURRECTIONS
6. omusa.org, Operation Mobilization, 116.

CHAPTER 6. A TRANSFORMED HEART/A COVETOUS HEART
7. *Crippled Tom*, childrensbibleclub.com (Milton, FL), 126.

8. http://www.ptl.org, 147.

CHAPTER 7. THE THREE MINI-MIRACLES
9. Wallace, Ronald, *Elijah and Elisha*. (Edinburgh, Oliver & Boyd, 1957), 154.

10. Eareckson, Joni, *Joni*. (Grand Rapids, Zondervan, 2001), 165.

CHAPTER 8. IN TIMES OF FAMINE
11. Cowman, Lettie, *Streams in the Dessert*. (Grand Rapids, Zondervan: 2008), 194.

CHAPTER 9. VICTORY
12. Webster, Irene, *Sensei*. (NY, Harper Row, 1965), 210.

CPSIA information can be obtained
at www.ICGtesting.com
Printed in the USA
JSHW010748140722
28077JS00004B/96